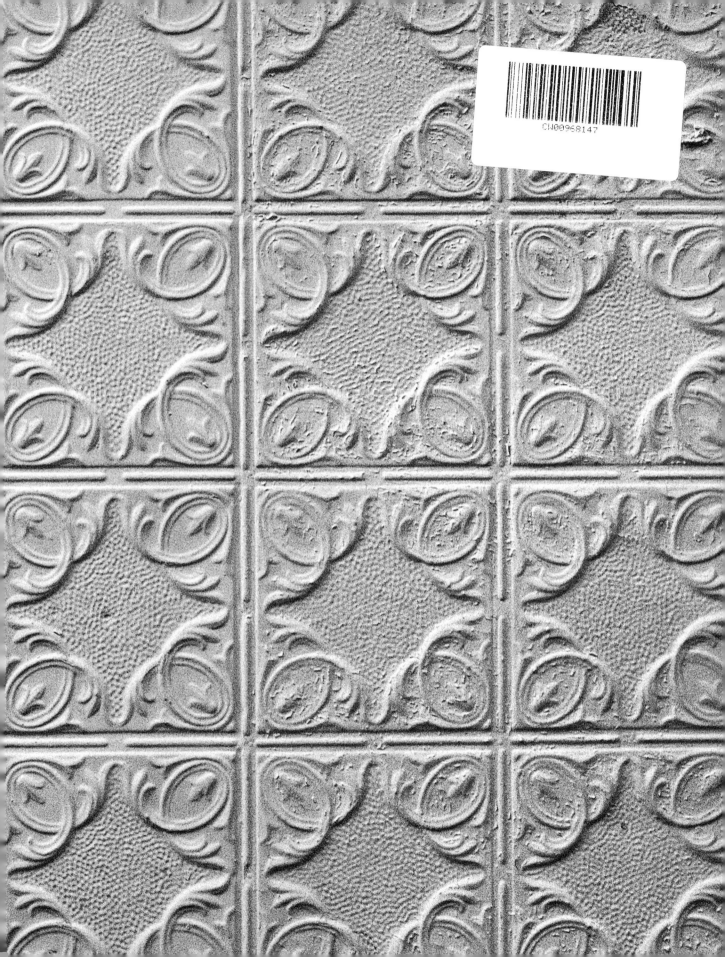

BROOKLYN RUSTIC

BROOKLYN RUSTIC

Simple Food for Sophisticated Palates

BRYAN CALVERT

with Tammy Walker

LITTLE, BROWN AND COMPANY
NEW YORK BOSTON LONDON

Little, Brown and Company
Hachette Book Group
1290 Avenue of the Americas, New York, NY 10104
littlebrown.com

First Edition: June 2016

Little, Brown and Company is a division of Hachette Book Group, Inc. The Little, Brown name and logo are trademarks of Hachette Book Group, Inc.

The publisher is not responsible for websites (or their content) that are not owned by the publisher.

The Hachette Speakers Bureau provides a wide range of authors for speaking events. To find out more, go to hachettespeakersbureau.com or call (866) 376-6591.

DESIGN BY Laura Palese

PHOTOGRAPHIC DIRECTION by Deborah Williamson

Photographic credits listed on page 296

ISBN 978-0-316-38040-9
Library of Congress Control Number: 2015960012

10 9 8 7 6 5 4 3 2 1

IM

Printed in China

*Eating with the fullest pleasure—pleasure, that is,
that does not depend on ignorance—is perhaps the profoundest
enactment of our connection with the world.*

WENDELL BERRY

CONTENTS

KALE

Baby Kale and Quinoa Salad with Almonds,
Roasted Garlic, and Poached Eggs 56

Kale and Ricotta Panisse 59

Black Kale and Cabbage Salad 60

CORN

Corn Broth 63

Corn Soup with Oysters, Pickled Corn,
and Tarragon 64

Roasted Corn and Duck Confit Salad 68

ONIONS

Spring Onion Soup with Pecorino
and Bacon 71

Cipollini Onion Brûlée with
Balsamic Vinegar and Rosemary 72

Leek Confit 73

Venison and Ramp Stew 74

Roasted Garlic Puree 77

BEANS

Three Legume Crostinis 78

Summer Beans with Bagna Cauda 81

Crispy Chickpeas with Rosemary 82

EGGPLANT

Grilled Eggplant with Merguez
and Spearmint 85

Eggplant Fries with Curry Aioli 86

Smoky Eggplant Puree with
Roasted Broccoli and Ricotta Salata 89

MUSHROOMS

Mushroom, Walnut, and Fennel Salad
with Parmigiano 90

Mushroom and Arugula Buckwheat Crepes 93

Mushrooms and Fennel
en Papillote 95

SQUASH

Summer Squash with Feta, Cured Olives, Chickpeas,
and Nasturtiums 97

Goat Cheese Gnocchi with Basil, Lemon,
and Baby Summer Squash 98

Ratatouille with Baked Duck Eggs 101

Jerked Butternut Squash 103

Delicata Squash with Honey and Red Pepper Flakes 104

Spaghetti Squash with Sage and Maple Syrup 107

Baby Blue Hubbard Squash Soup with Blue Cheese
and Pickled Pears 109

CARROTS

Quick-Pickled Cumin Carrots 112

Roasted Carrots, Parsnips, and Belgian Endive
with Curry and Currants 113

Sherry-Glazed Carrots and Radishes 114

CABBAGE

Napa Cabbage Slaw with Sriracha Aioli 117

Baby Bok Choy with Roasted Red Pepper Sauce 118

Roasted Brussels Sprouts with Apples,
Pistachios, and Bacon 121

BEETS

Beet Risotto with Goat Cheese and Dill 122

Golden Beet Broth with Goat Cheese
and Beet Dumplings 125

Baby Beet Salad with Tangerines and
Oil-Cured Olives 127

SWISS CHARD

Creamed Swiss Chard with
Red Wine Shallots 129

Rainbow Chard with Lentils, Apricots,
and Green Curry 130

Swiss Chard Pastilla with Smoked Duck
and Currants 132

TURNIPS

Kohlrabi, Apple, and Hijiki Slaw 135

Tokyo Turnips and Pears with Cardamom
Vinaigrette 136

Roasted Rutabaga with Grapefruit, Avocado,
and Basil 138

CELERY ROOT

Celery Root Salad with Pancetta,
Walnut Mayonnaise, and Lovage 139

Celery Root Soup with Trout, Pear, and Curry Oil 143

Celery Root and Potato Gratin with Fresh Horseradish 144

SUNCHOKES

Roasted Sunchokes with Watercress
and Hazelnuts 147

Sunchoke-Almond Soup 148

POTATOES

Crushed Yukon Gold Potatoes with
Garlic and Parsley 151

Potatoes Dauphine with Scallions
and Manchego 152

Green Goddess Potato Salad 155

PART TWO

SEAFOOD

SHELLFISH

Roasted Oysters with Celery, Bacon, and
Fresh Horseradish 158

Pickled Oysters 161

Three Oyster Sauces 162

Sautéed Shrimp with Harissa Broth 167

Chinatown Shrimp 168

Shrimp and Kimchi Fritters 170

Stove-Smoked Scallops and Mussels with Pasta 173

Seared Scallops with Roasted Cauliflower
and Olive Puree 174

Scallops Marinated with Horseradish and
Lemon Thyme 177

FISH

Black Cod with Figs and Fennel 180

Crab-Crusted Halibut 183

Cured Salmon with Arugula, Beets, and
Horseradish-Chive Cream 184

Striped Bass Poached in Corn Broth 186

Spring Onion–Stuffed Brook Trout with Pine Nuts 189

Grilled Branzino with Fennel and
Olive Escabeche 190

Black Sea Bass with Pepita Crust 192

Cod with Sweet Peppers and Spicy Sausage 193

PART THREE

MEAT AND POULTRY

EGGS

Soft Scrambled Eggs with Chives and Brioche 198

Deviled Eggs Three Ways 199

Baked Farmer's Eggs 202

POULTRY

Tandoori Chicken 204

Turmeric Chicken with Artichokes and Basil Yogurt 206

Savory-Stuffed Skillet Chicken with
Lemon-Miso Sauce 209

PORK

Glazed Braised Pork Belly with Beans and Fennel 212

Blackberry-Basted Pork Tenderloin 214

Cider-Glazed Pork Chops with Sage and Apples 216

Pork Loin Crusted with Pecans and Mustard 218

BEEF

Balsamic-Soy Marinated Hanger Steak 220

Dry-Rubbed Porterhouse with Tamarind Steak Sauce 223

LAMB

Pomegranate-Braised Lamb Shanks 225

Lamb Sirloin Crusted with Cocoa and Cumin 228

Lamb and Goat Cheese Pasties 231

THE BROOKLYN RUSTIC WAY

WITH THE RIGHT APPROACH, anyone can turn an average meal into an inspired one. That's what this book offers: a straightforward way of cooking that makes your food more flavorful and your time at the market and in the kitchen more rewarding.

I call my approach "Brooklyn Rustic" because it mixes country simplicity with urban complexity. If you're like me, you love the food that you're familiar with, but you seek a little adventure in your life. My recipes show you how to begin with familiar ingredients and dishes and easily make them intriguing with the hint of something new, fresh, or different that's often right under your nose. This is old-world cooking that comes to life with modern ingredients.

I cook this way in Brooklyn, but you can and should cook this food anywhere. These recipes are built on staples that are available nationwide and use simple techniques that anyone can master. (If you want proof in a single recipe, try my tomato salad on page 51.) I tested them in my home kitchen using modest equipment, and backed those tests up with the experiences of friends and family.

I also include practical tips on approach, technique, and presentation to give you confidence, as well as essays about why I make the choices I do. Simple habits like shopping thoughtfully, taking a minute to finish a dish, or setting up your kitchen in a sensible way can make a big difference in your food and how much fun you have preparing it.

Because cooking and eating are so central to our lives, I also encourage you to think about the role of food in your world. For me, cooking the Brooklyn Rustic way actually means *living* the Brooklyn Rustic way: finding ways to listen to the rhythms of the natural world amid the tumult of a big city. That juxtaposition feeds me creatively and generates energy and ideas.

I've cooked in four-star kitchens and over campfires in the woods. What makes a great meal is not technique or formality. It's the experience of sharing something handmade and witnessing the pleasure it brings. This is why I cook. With this book I return to the true purpose of preparing a meal: to fill your belly and to give something you created to people you love.

THE STORY OF JAMES

When I moved to the Prospect Heights neighborhood of Brooklyn in the mid-1990s, I thought Brooklyn was where you lived only if you couldn't afford Manhattan, not a destination of its own. I was wrong. Brooklyn has always had an attitude of independence, and exploded with a community of artists, craftsmen, and chefs seeking relief from the formality and expense of Manhattan.

I landed here after traveling around as a culinary journeyman, living out of my backpack as I bounced from the city to the countryside. I loved how the beauty and tempo of bucolic life contrasted with the energy and diversity of the city. As a cook in Manhattan, I didn't get to experience big skies and fresh air, but I soon discovered Brooklyn was a mash-up of those urban and rustic pleasures.

Around the same time, talented chefs began drawing attention to unique nooks on unheard-of avenues in Brooklyn. Untethered from high rents and demanding investors, they found the freedom to cook what they wanted. Farmers' markets sprang up. Community and rooftop gardens sprouted in industrial neighborhoods. The pioneer spirit took root.

My moment came when the restaurant I was living above went up for sale. I knew it was time. (It had been a bodega with bulletproof glass surrounding the cash register a few years earlier.) I had opened restaurants before, but with deep-pocketed investors, veteran restaurateurs, and teams of experts. This time it had to be mom-and-pop style—personal and hands-on. It was a daunting undertaking. But one day, poking around the new space, I discovered an original tin ceiling from the turn of the century hidden under a cheap drop ceiling. It was perfectly preserved, and at that point I knew everything was going to be all right.

James opened on June 15, 2008. It is named after my great-grandfather, who was a chef at the turn of the twentieth century in New York, around the time our building was erected. We were busy from the first day. Guests felt all the hands-on attention my business partner, Deborah Williamson, and I put into James, and they seemed to like what we had done. It felt personal and genuine. That's the reason why people cherish little corner neighborhood restaurants all over the world, and the reason why our kind of Brooklyn restaurant has become so popular.

Three months after we opened, Lehman Brothers filed for bankruptcy and business began to dwindle along with the economy. The most impressive dishes became the ones that weren't selling. I realized, with Deborah's help, that the kind of food I liked—the dishes that could be eaten frequently and enjoyed consistently—was selling the most, not the "special-occasion" dishes that I thought I had to cook.

As the economy spiraled downward, our real customers emerged. They wanted thoughtful, uncomplicated food made from quality ingredients and served in a comfortable atmosphere. To accommodate their tastes and wallets without skimping on quality, I had to ask myself hard questions. What if I use a less expensive cut of meat? Does this dish really need two sauces? Am I showcasing the ingredients or obscuring them?

My strategy shifted from what I should add to the plate to what I should take off.

HOW WE EAT IS WHO WE ARE

Simpler food means fewer cooks, fewer ingredients, and lower costs. Fewer ingredients means less waste and a more efficient kitchen. We could charge less without sacrificing quality and have more money to buy better ingredients. It was a good scenario.

Many small businesses in Brooklyn grew with the same approach. Thoughtful, handmade products emerged from independent entrepreneurs who wanted to live their own lives and do things their own way. Everything from pickles to clothing appeared: handcrafted, sustainable, owner-operated, and personal. A diverse but definitive style was born, more of an attitude than a single specific approach. That's Brooklyn Rustic, and it's how I cook and live.

This way of cooking has taught me to embrace diversity and express my values through the choices I make. What we eat, where we shop, and how we cook are daily experiences that define who we are and what we believe. Witnessing and encouraging the beauty in our communities gives a reprieve from the stress of modern life. For me, it all starts with food. Respecting simplicity in ingredients and craftsmanship allows us to experience wonder at our surroundings—whatever and wherever they might be.

PART ONE

VEGETABLES

A Cook's Garden

With only a little effort, you can grow
key ingredients that make a big difference.

It is incredibly difficult to grow most of your own food. I know—I tried it one summer in a 3,000-square-foot garden in the southern Berkshires. I worked 12 hours a day, 7 days a week—and was only moderately successful. I had a blast, but not much time for anything else.

You don't need to go to that extreme to reap the benefits of a cook's garden. Whether yours sits on a small windowsill or roams across a huge backyard, the best investment of your space, funds, and time is in culinary herbs and aromatic plants.

Hardy herbs	*Less hardy, but easy to grow*	*Vegetables*
Anise hyssop	Basil (all varieties)	Bronze fennel
Bay leaf	Chervil	Celery
Lemon balm	Chives	Cherry tomatoes
Lemongrass	Cilantro	Green onions
Lemon thyme	Culantro	Kale
Lemon verbena	Dill	Mushrooms
Lovage	French tarragon	Radishes
Mexican tarragon	Nasturtium leaves and flowers	Peppers (small varieties)
Mint (all varieties)	Parsley	Vietnamese garlic chives
Rosemary	Sorrel	
Sage	Summer savory	
Sweet marjoram	Tarragon	
Thyme		

I've learned the hard way that some things are better left to the farmers. A constant supply of fresh-picked lemon thyme will go a lot further in your recipes than a head of lettuce, and it's a lot easier to grow. And if you've ever bought a bunch of fresh herbs, used only a few springs, and watched the rest of the bunch go brown, then you already see the benefit of picking only what you need, when you need it.

Herbs can be dried and stored, and if you live in a cold climate, there are perennial varieties you can bring indoors for the winter, like rosemary, thyme, and sage. (I have the most success with organic seedlings, which I buy at the farmers' market or online.)

Even if you think you don't have the space, look around. One neighbor kept a bunch of old toilets on the stoop filled with herbs and vegetables! I rummage through junk to find

treasures to transform into plant containers. Just make sure the material is safe to use—you don't want to grow herbs in a lead bucket—and if you're using a backyard plot, test the soil for contaminants (see Buying, page 294).

Try something really different and grow your own mushrooms. Many different home-growing mushroom kits and spores are available. I've had the most success with shiitakes and oyster mushrooms. They can be grown indoors, or outside under the right conditions, and a healthy colony can produce multiple crops. Your home-grown mushrooms can be eaten fresh or dried and stored for long periods of time.

Grow something. Experiencing an ingredient's journey from seed to plate will make you appreciate food in a new way.

HANDLING FRESH HERBS

The best way to preserve the flavor and longevity of fresh herbs is to store them the way they grow on the plant: leaves up, stems down, with a little space to breathe. I keep them in recycled glass jars sealed with airtight lids. If the herbs are freshly picked, extra moisture hastens decay. But if the herbs seem thirsty, place a damp paper towel in the bottom of the jar. If they are wilted when you bring them home, give them a quick rinse in very cold water and shake off any excess moisture—or better yet, find a purveyor with fresher produce.

CUTTING HERBS

Cutting herbs properly is essential to preserving their delicate flavor and vibrant appearance. *Chiffonade*, a French term translating to "little ribbons," is the ideal way to cut delicate leafy herbs. Instead of chopping and pounding the poor plants into the cutting board with your knife, loosely roll and slice them into fine ribbons. This way of cutting herbs and leafy greens makes the difference between bruised, crushed leaves that deteriorate quickly and attractive green ribbons that hold up over time. Using a sharp knife and slicing away from you puts less weight on the leaves and doesn't bruise them like chopping up and down will.

{ ESSAY CONTINUES }

PRESERVING HERBS

Plants, including herbs, grow at their own pace. Sometimes I'm fortunate enough to grow a large crop during the summer and fall. To preserve them for the seasons ahead, I employ two approaches: dry and wet.

For hardy herbs like rosemary, sage, and thyme, drying works well and the strong flavors hold up over time. Trim the branches and hang them leaves down, branches not touching, in a dark, cool, dry place with good ventilation for a few days. Make sure they are completely dry to avoid molding. Remove the leaves and store them in airtight jars. Toss the dried stems on the barbecue for a little extra smoky flavor.

For delicate herbs like basil, mint, parsley, and cilantro, I make oil-based sauces like chimichurri (page 20), pistou (page 19), and pesto (page 23) and freeze them in small batches. The oil captures their taste and aroma and will keep for a few months in the freezer.

Infusing vinegars with herbs is another quick way to capture their flavors. Fully submerge a few fresh herb sprigs in a sealed bottle of vinegar, and the vinegar will take on the flavors of the herbs in a few days. The herbs must always be fully submerged in the vinegar to prevent them from molding. Use delicate herbs (basil, cilantro, French tarragon, lemon thyme) with lighter vinegars like white wine or rice vinegar, and robust herbs (rosemary, sage, thyme) with stronger vinegars like sherry, red wine, or balsamic vinegar. You can also use leftover wine in place of vinegar to make a cooking wine that's great for pan sauces. ❊

SHALLOT-HERB PISTOU

PISTOU IS PESTO'S COUSIN, minus the pine nuts. Any combination of herbs works here, so I usually head out to my herb garden and snip a few handfuls of whatever is available. It's not a make-it-or-break-it step, but I blanch the herbs before blending them. That step preserves their vibrant green color that could otherwise turn brown from the acid in the tomatoes and lemon juice. Stir pistou into soups, toss it into a salad or pasta, or spread it on toasted bread for sandwiches.

MAKES ABOUT 2 CUPS · ACTIVE: 20 MIN · TOTAL: 20 MIN

1 cup lightly packed fresh basil leaves

1 cup lightly packed fresh chervil leaves

2 teaspoons fresh tarragon leaves

1 cup extra-virgin olive oil, chilled, plus
    1 tablespoon

1 teaspoon fine sea salt

Freshly ground black pepper

1 shallot, finely diced

1 plum tomato, seeds removed and diced

Small pinch of red pepper flakes

Finely grated zest and juice of 1 lemon

Chill the blender container in the freezer for a few minutes. (You can use a food processor, but I prefer a blender when working with only a cup or two.) Meanwhile, bring a pot of salted water to a boil, and prepare a medium bowl of ice water.

Add the basil, chervil, and tarragon to the boiling water for 10 seconds. Drain the herbs into a small strainer and dunk it into the ice water for 10 seconds. Lift the strainer out and squeeze any excess water out of the herbs.

In the cold blender, blend the herbs, the 1 cup olive oil, the salt, and two turns of black pepper on high speed until the herbs are finely minced, stopping to scrape down the sides with a spatula if necessary.

Pour into a glass bowl and stir in the shallot, tomato, and red pepper flakes until well combined. Stir in the lemon zest and juice. Cover the top with the remaining 1 tablespoon olive oil to prevent the surface from discoloring. Refrigerate in an airtight container for up to 4 days. (If not using right away, wait to stir in the lemon zest and juice until right before using.)

SWEET MARJORAM CHIMICHURRI

EASY-TO-GROW SWEET MARJORAM IS similar to oregano, but it has a milder sweet flavor and subtle spiciness. Paired with fresh parsley, it makes a bold, tangy chimichurri that's great for seared meats and grilled vegetables. Put out a bowl of the chunky sauce at your next barbecue and slather it on everything.

MAKES ABOUT 2 CUPS · ACTIVE: 15 MIN · TOTAL: 30 MIN

2 tablespoons sherry vinegar

1 tablespoon honey

½ cup extra-virgin olive oil

2 garlic cloves, minced

1 small shallot, finely chopped

1 fresh or pickled jalapeño, seeds removed and finely chopped

¼ teaspoon sweet paprika

¾ teaspoon fine sea salt

Freshly ground black pepper

¼ cup lightly packed fresh sweet marjoram leaves, finely chopped

1 teaspoon fresh thyme or lemon thyme, finely chopped

1½ cups lightly packed fresh flat-leaf parsley, cut into ribbons

In a bowl, whisk together the vinegar, honey, olive oil, garlic, shallot, jalapeño, paprika, salt and two turns of pepper. Stir in the marjoram, thyme, and parsley and let sit for 15 minutes to allow the herb flavor to intensify. Taste and adjust the seasoning as needed. Refrigerate in an airtight container for up to 4 days, or freeze for up to 2 weeks.

*Buttery Lemon–
Basil Pesto*

*Shallot–Herb
Pistou*

*Lime–Cilantro
Butter*

*Sweet Marjoram
Chimichurri*

LIME-CILANTRO BUTTER

THIS BRIGHT, ZESTY COMPOUND butter is every grilled vegetable's dream, especially corn on the cob. Use it to pump up steak, rub on roasted chicken, or sauté shrimp.

MAKES ABOUT ½ CUP · ACTIVE: 15 MIN · TOTAL: 1 HR 45 MIN

1 stick (8 tablespoons) unsalted
   butter, softened

¼ teaspoon finely grated lime zest

1 tablespoon freshly squeezed
   lime juice

1 tablespoon chopped fresh
   flat-leaf parsley

1 tablespoon chopped fresh cilantro

½ teaspoon fine sea salt

½ teaspoon crushed pink peppercorns

Using a fork or the back of a spoon, smash together all of the ingredients in a bowl until evenly combined. Drop the butter onto an 8 x 11-inch sheet of parchment paper and shape it into a log about 6 inches long. Wrap it tightly and twist the ends. Refrigerate until firm, at least 1 hour and 30 minutes. It will keep in the refrigerator for up to 5 days or in the freezer for up to 2 weeks. If freezing, wrap a layer of plastic wrap around the parchment paper.

BUTTERY LEMON-BASIL PESTO

SEVERAL FRESH BASIL VARIETIES are available at most farmers' markets in the summer—cinnamon basil, Genovese basil, Thai basil, purple basil, and others. They range from sweet to spicy, intense to lightly floral, and give you countless ways to switch up a classic pesto recipe. I like to add lemon basil for a citrusy dimension. If you don't grow it and can't find it, just double the amount of bright, floral Genovese basil, which is similar to the regular Italian sweet basil readily available at most grocery stores. If you're wondering why there's butter here . . . well, why not? It adds creaminess and richness for an extra decadent pesto.

MAKES ABOUT 1 CUP · ACTIVE: 15 MIN · TOTAL: 15 MIN

1 cup lightly packed fresh lemon basil leaves

1 cup lightly packed fresh basil leaves

½ cup extra-virgin olive oil, chilled, plus 1 tablespoon

2 tablespoons pine nuts, toasted

2 garlic cloves, smashed

3 tablespoons unsalted butter, softened

1 teaspoon fine sea salt

¾ cup freshly grated Parmigiano-Reggiano

Chill the blender container in the freezer for a few minutes.

In the cold blender, puree both types of basil, the ½ cup olive oil, the pine nuts, garlic, butter, and salt on high speed until smooth, scraping down the sides with a spatula if necessary. This should take only a minute or two. Be sure not to run the blender for too long, so the pesto doesn't heat up.

Pour into a glass bowl and stir in the cheese. Cover the top with the remaining 1 tablespoon olive oil to prevent the surface from discoloring. Cover with an airtight lid and refrigerate for up to 4 days.

CHIVE OIL

I REACH FOR THIS bright green finishing oil to drizzle on soups, toss into salads, or add color to a serving plate. It adds a subtle chive flavor, not a knock-you-over-the head onion pungency, so it works in a lot of contexts. If you grow chives, make a few batches and freeze the oil in ice cube trays.

MAKES ABOUT 1 CUP · ACTIVE: 15 MIN · TOTAL: 1 HR 15 MIN

1 cup extra-virgin olive oil
1 bunch chives, finely chopped

Pinch of fine sea salt

In a small pot, heat the olive oil, chives, and salt over high heat until the oil starts to bubble a little, about 2 minutes. Immediately transfer the mixture to a blender and blend on high speed for 2 minutes. Pour into a small glass bowl and chill for at least 1 hour and up to 1 day (if chilling for more than an hour, cover it with plastic wrap after it cools).

Strain through a fine-mesh sieve set over a bowl. Refrigerate the oil for up to 1 week, or freeze for up to 1 month.

A Pantry Full of Mason Jars

If you want a great local tomato in January, you're not going to get it at the grocery store. That's where preserving—the process of locking in the flavors of ingredients at their peak to enjoy them in the future—comes in.

I cook preserves to rediscover the natural rhythms of the seasons and avoid the tasteless ingredients we see all year in the supermarkets. In this era of convenient plastic-wrapped food, it is deeply gratifying to open up your pantry door to shelves of colorful glass jars—a treasure of homemade provisions to rely on. When it's cold and dreary outside, you won't get the bright acidic-sweet hit of summer from a pale supermarket tomato that tastes like a tennis ball. But you'll love pulling a jar of home-canned tomatoes from your shelf.

Pickled, preserved, and fermented products have become a trademark of the Brooklyn food scene, where cooks and artisans embrace the traditions established here by new immigrants centuries ago. Preservation was a necessity before refrigerated transportation and seasonless food. Today, choosing to preserve the old-fashioned way is an act of respect that showcases the best qualities of ingredients. The goal is to take advantage of ripe fruits and vegetables when they are in abundance. Most of the food we cook at home is eaten right away, but preserving slows things down. It forces us to patiently wait for flavors to develop in Mother Nature's own good time.

There are several methods for easy home preservation, and all involve heat or acid and creating an airtight seal. Because you're extending the usable life of food, it's essential to do this properly. Otherwise, you can waste a lot of time or even make yourself sick. At the height of summer, invest in some canning equipment and a book that shows you how to do it (there are plenty of great ones). Producing your first Mason jars of preserves will be a good afternoon of work, but once you taste the first fruits of your labor, you'll be hooked. ❧

CHILLED WATERMELON
AND LEMON VERBENA SOUP

CHILLED FRUIT SOUPS ARE a refreshing way to conclude a meal. This version showcases fresh watermelon in three different textures, but to simplify it you can skip the frozen, shaved watermelon granita, or make it the day before. If you do freeze the watermelon ahead of time, move it to the refrigerator half an hour before you scrape it, to soften the ice. Lemon verbena is key here—it has all the flavor and fragrance of lemons without any of their acidity.

SERVES 4 TO 6 · ACTIVE: 30 MIN · TOTAL: 2 HR 30 MIN

1 ripe seedless watermelon (about 5 pounds), flesh cut into ¼-inch cubes

¼ cup fresh lemon verbena leaves, plus 4 leaves for garnish

¼ cup light floral honey, such as acacia

Finely grated zest and juice of 2 limes

1 teaspoon extra-virgin olive oil, preferably a young, fruity variety

Select the firmest, most perfectly square cubes (about one-third of the total watermelon), place them in a bowl, and chill in the refrigerator.

Add half of the remaining cubed watermelon to a blender along with the lemon verbena and blend until smooth. Pour into a bowl and chill in the refrigerator.

Add the remaining half of the cubed watermelon to the blender with the honey, lime zest, and lime juice and puree. Pour into a shallow glass or nonreactive casserole dish and freeze until frozen, 2 to 4 hours.

To serve, divide the reserved chilled watermelon cubes evenly among four chilled soup bowls. Pour the chilled watermelon–lemon verbena soup over the cubes.

Using a fork, scrape the frozen watermelon mixture back and forth in different directions until a rough sorbet-like texture is created. Scoop a dollop of watermelon ice into each bowl and drizzle ¼ teaspoon olive oil in the center. Garnish with a lemon verbena leaf and serve immediately.

BITTER GREENS

with Dates, Sesame, and Warm Goat Cheese

BITTER GREENS LIKE ARUGULA, radicchio, chicory, and endive are every bit as salad-friendly as spinach once you know how to handle their pungent, peppery bite. A little sweetness in the form of a date-based vinaigrette takes the edge off, and a few rounds of pan-fried goat cheese further soften the greens' assertiveness and bring all the rich flavors together.

SERVES 4 TO 6 · ACTIVE: 20 MIN · TOTAL: 20 MIN

8 pitted Medjool dates

1 large egg white

Fine sea salt

1 cup bread crumbs, preferably panko (Japanese-style bread crumbs)

2 tablespoons chopped fresh chives

½ cup sesame seeds, toasted

Freshly ground black pepper

1 (8-ounce) log goat cheese, cut into 8 rounds

6 tablespoons extra-virgin olive oil

3 tablespoons toasted sesame oil

¼ cup sherry vinegar

¼ cup freshly squeezed orange juice

Freshly ground black pepper

2 bunches arugula, large stems removed and leaves coarsely chopped (about 3 cups)

1 medium head radicchio, quartered lengthwise and thinly sliced (about 2 cups)

2 heads Belgian endive, ends trimmed and leaves thinly sliced (about 2 cups)

Cut the dates into small pieces and soak them in warm water to cover for 10 minutes.

Lightly whisk the egg white with 1 tablespoon cold water and a pinch of salt.

In a shallow dish, combine the bread crumbs, 1 tablespoon of the chives, 2 tablespoons of the sesame seeds, a pinch of salt, and two turns of black pepper.

Dip the goat cheese rounds in the egg whites, then dredge in the bread crumb mixture, thoroughly coating each piece. Refrigerate the breaded cheese for at least 15 minutes so that the cheese firms up.

Drain the date pieces and add them to a blender along with 3 tablespoons of the olive oil, the sesame oil, sherry vinegar, orange juice, and ¼ cup of the sesame seeds. Blend until a smooth, fairly thick vinaigrette forms, about 3 minutes. Season with salt and pepper to taste.

In a large sauté pan, heat the remaining 3 tablespoons olive oil over medium heat. Add the cheese rounds and brown on each side for about 1 minute. Transfer them to a paper towel–lined plate to soak up any excess oil.

In a large serving bowl, toss the arugula, radicchio, endive, remaining 2 tablespoons sesame seeds, and remaining 1 tablespoon chives with the vinaigrette until everything is coated. Top the salad with the warm goat cheese rounds and serve.

BABY SPINACH SALAD

with Mushrooms and Pine Nuts

THE BEST TIME FOR baby spinach is the spring and fall, when the weather is cool and the leaves are the most tender. Thanks to the shiitakes, Parmigiano, and roasted onions, this salad can be a meal in itself—but it's never a bad idea to throw in a little bacon or to top it with a poached egg.

SERVES 4 · ACTIVE: 15 MIN · TOTAL: 15 MIN

¼ cup pine nuts

Fine sea salt

1 tablespoon extra-virgin olive oil

6 ounces shiitake mushrooms, stemmed and thinly sliced

1 teaspoon finely chopped fresh lemon thyme

Freshly ground black pepper

10 ounces baby spinach, stemmed

¼ cup freshly grated Parmigiano-Reggiano

1 teaspoon finely grated lemon zest

2 tablespoons Balsamic Vinaigrette (page 287)

8 small pieces Cipollini Onion Brûlée with Balsamic Vinegar and Rosemary (page 72)

Toast the pine nuts in a dry skillet over medium heat, stirring, until they're light brown, 3 to 5 minutes. Lightly season with salt and transfer to a small bowl.

In the same skillet, heat the olive oil over medium heat and cook the mushrooms until lightly tender, about 3 minutes. Stir in the thyme, a pinch of salt, and two turns of black pepper.

In a large salad bowl, toss together the spinach, mushrooms, cheese, toasted pine nuts, and lemon zest. Add the balsamic vinaigrette and toss. Garnish with the cipollini onions.

GRILLED RADICCHIO

with Anchovy Cream

NEXT TIME YOU BARBECUE, toss some radicchio on the grill. Its sturdy, reddish purple leaves grill beautifully, becoming tender and less bitter. Anchovies, which contribute bold umami flavor with little effort from you, stand up to bitterness of the radicchio. The sweet-and-sour notes of the balsamic vinegar make this powerhouse of flavor well suited to the smoky char of the barbecue.

SERVES 4 TO 6 · ACTIVE: 20 MIN · TOTAL: 30 MIN

4 oil-packed anchovies

⅓ cup sour cream

1 tablespoon finely grated Parmigiano-Reggiano

1 tablespoon freshly squeezed lemon juice

1 teaspoon Roasted Garlic Puree (page 77), or ½ teaspoon chopped garlic

3 tablespoons extra-virgin olive oil

Fine sea salt

4 small heads radicchio

Fresh black pepper

1 to 2 tablespoons Balsamic Reduction (page 287; optional)

Prepare a hot grill and oil the grill rack.

Combine the anchovies, sour cream, cheese, lemon juice, garlic puree, 1 tablespoon of the olive oil, and salt to taste in a blender and puree until smooth, about 1 minute.

Remove any loose outer leaves from the radicchio heads and line a serving platter with them. Cut the heads into quarters lengthwise, keeping the stem intact so the wedges hold together.

In a large bowl, gently toss the wedges with the remaining 2 tablespoons olive oil and salt and pepper to taste. Grill both sides of the radicchio until slightly charred and tender, 2 to 4 minutes per side. Transfer to the serving platter and drizzle with the anchovy cream and balsamic reduction, if using.

MELTED ROMAINE

THE ROOTS OF THIS recipe are from the famed New York restaurant Delmonico's, which ruled the city's culinary scene in the 1800s. They treated lettuce as they did everything else back in the day: as a vehicle for butter. While I've lightened it up, this is still a luscious way to dig in to some greens. For the full effect, serve the romaine wedges intact in the dish they were baked in. You can also make this on a hot grill—just brush the lettuce with melted butter first and grill for a few minutes on each side.

SERVES 4 TO 6 · ACTIVE: 5 MIN · TOTAL: 15 MIN

4 tablespoons unsalted butter, cubed

2 medium heads romaine lettuce

Fine sea salt

½ cup finely grated aged Gruyère cheese or Parmigiano-Reggiano

2 tablespoons chopped fresh chives

1 tablespoon capers, rinsed and finely chopped

1 tablespoon finely grated lemon zest

2 teaspoons freshly squeezed lemon juice

Freshly ground black pepper

Preheat the oven to 425°F.

Put the butter in a large cast-iron griddle or roasting pan and place in the oven until the butter starts to foam, about 5 minutes.

While the butter is melting, remove any tough outer leaves from the heads of lettuce and slice off any brown parts from the root ends. Quarter the heads of lettuce lengthwise, keeping the root intact so the long wedges stay together. Season both sides of the lettuce wedges with salt to taste.

Arrange the lettuce cut side down in one layer in the pan and bake for 5 minutes. Turn the wedges cut side up and continue cooking until the lettuce wilts and the butter slightly browns, about 5 more minutes. Remove from the oven. Sprinkle with the cheese, chives, capers, lemon zest, juice, and four turns of black pepper. Serve immediately.

You Are Not Alone

When one tugs at a single thing in nature, he finds it attached to the rest of the world.
JOHN MUIR

Cooking is just one event of many that contributes to creating food.
The success of what you cook is affected by its relationship to everything involved in it: the soil it grew in, the grass an animal ate, the person who picked the vegetables, the sun, your mood, the cookware you use, the plate you present it on, and the environment you serve it in. We are all pieces of a large ecology: Each small piece related to the others makes the whole. The process of developing flavor starts long before you have the ingredient in your kitchen. Making a connection to the source of the food you eat makes the act of cooking more meaningful, and can be a way to re-center your view of the world.

When I started to grow a lot of my own vegetables, I learned patience and humility. There was no other option. I had to accept the wildness of my garden: No matter how much effort I exert, I have limited control. The journey an ingredient takes to get to your plate—growth, harvest, transport—affects the flavor and success of the dish being prepared.

I know the farmers who grew the tomatoes in the salad that *The New York Times* food critic liked so much (Jeffrey Frank and Kirstin Illick from Liberty Gardens), and I feel like they did most of the work. Cultivating awareness and respect of where your food comes from and connecting with that source is key.

Do you have to commit all your time to this? No—but try it one meal at a time. You'll improve what you eat, and that change may lead to other changes, because food is one big part of the ecology of our lives. If you ever feel disconnected, uncentered, out of whack, look at what you're eating. Maybe you can bring yourself back to center by connecting what you eat with who you are—or who you want to be. I want to be empathetic, thoughtful, respectful, full of love, and connected to the world around me. The choices I make about what to cook and eat are a part of who I am.

Fostering these relationships doesn't need to be difficult. You don't have to grow your own food, visit the farm, or know the farmer. Be realistic and patient. Start with one potted herb on your windowsill. When you shop at the supermarket, check to see if their policies are in line with your needs and beliefs. Get to know a little about whom you buy your food from, whether it is a national chain or the farmer down the road. This act rebuilds your connection with what you eat. That connection creates love and respect for food, and that respect makes you a more thoughtful and successful cook. ❧

SAUTÉED CUCUMBERS

with Spearmint, Cilantro, and Lime

I LIKE TO TAKE an uncommon approach to common vegetables because it often opens up culinary possibilities. I also explore the cuisines of other cultures to get a different point of view on familiar ingredients. We eat cucumbers raw or pickled almost all the time, but here I sauté them, as is more common in Asian cuisine.

This is a quick way to make cucumbers into a versatile condiment or side dish for barbecue, grilled fish, or anything spicy. If the cukes are small and tender, leave the skin on for more color and flavor. I prefer spearmint to peppermint for savory dishes like this one because its flavor is deeper and more complex.

SERVES 4 TO 6 · ACTIVE: 15 MIN · TOTAL: 15 MIN

1 tablespoon extra-virgin olive oil

2 large English cucumbers, seeded and cut into ½-inch dice (about 4 cups)

2 scallions, cut into ¼-inch pieces

1 teaspoon minced fresh ginger

2 tablespoons soy sauce or tamari

Finely grated zest and juice of 2 limes

¼ cup lightly packed fresh cilantro leaves, sliced, plus a few sprigs for serving

¼ cup lightly packed fresh spearmint or peppermint leaves, sliced, plus a few sprigs for serving

In a large sauté pan, heat the olive oil over high heat. Add the cucumbers without overcrowding the pan (cook in two batches, if necessary) and cook for 4 minutes, stirring frequently, until softened but still crunchy.

Add the scallions and ginger and cook for another minute. Pour in the soy sauce and lime juice and cook until the liquid is almost gone but the cucumbers are still a little bit crunchy, about 1 minute. Remove from the heat.

Toss in the lime zest, cilantro, and spearmint. Serve hot with mint and cilantro sprigs as garnish. This can also be refrigerated until chilled and served as a cold salad.

CUCUMBER SOUP

with Crab, Basil, and Mint

LIGHT, REFRESHING, AND PACKED with flavor, this is an ideal start to a summer dinner. It should be served cold, so be careful not to over-blend the cucumbers—all that friction can warm the blender's contents and destroy the delicate melon-like flavor of the cucumbers. The soup can be made ahead of time and kept in the refrigerator, but you'll need to whisk it again just before serving because it will separate as it sits.

SERVES 4 · ACTIVE: 30 MIN · TOTAL: 30 MIN

For the soup:

1 pound seedless cucumbers

1 cup Vegetable Stock, chilled (page 292)

½ teaspoon mirin or honey

1½ teaspoons rice vinegar

Fine sea salt

For the crab:

¼ cup plain Greek yogurt

2 tablespoons Vegetable Stock (page 292)

1 teaspoon finely grated lime zest

1 teaspoon freshly squeezed lime juice

1 tablespoon extra-virgin olive oil, plus 2 teaspoons for serving

1 tablespoon sliced fresh basil

1 tablespoon sliced fresh mint, plus 4 sprigs for garnish

1 tablespoon sliced scallions

¼ teaspoon hot paprika, plus more for serving

Pinch of cayenne pepper

Pinch of freshly ground black pepper

8 ounces fresh peekytoe or jumbo lump crabmeat, picked free of shells, drained well

To make the soup: Peel ½ pound of the cucumbers and coarsely dice all of the cucumbers. Put the diced cucumbers, vegetable stock, mirin, rice vinegar, and a pinch of salt in a blender container/bowl. Cover and chill in the refrigerator, along with 4 empty soup bowls.

To make the crab: In a bowl, combine the yogurt, vegetable stock, lime zest and juice, 1 tablespoon of the olive oil, basil, mint, scallions, paprika, cayenne, and black pepper, and mix until smooth. Gently incorporate the crab, keeping it as chunky as possible.

Blend the chilled soup ingredients on high speed until smooth, about 2 minutes. Taste and adjust the seasoning as needed.

Divide the soup among the chilled serving bowls, and mound one-quarter of the crab mixture into each. Drizzle each serving with ½ teaspoon olive oil, dust with a pinch of paprika, and garnish with a sprig of mint. Serve immediately.

CUCUMBER AND WATERCRESS SALAD

with Dill and Wasabi

CUCUMBER SLICES TOSSED IN a bright, creamy, wasabi-spiked sauce make an easy, refreshing summer salad. Since they're used raw here, mild, sweet-tasting heirloom cucumbers are ideal. To add a cool, sweet element, toss chunks of watermelon into the mix. Store-bought wasabi is really just horseradish. Fresh wasabi is a pricier delicacy worth a try.

SERVES 4 TO 6 · ACTIVE: 15 MIN · TOTAL: 15 MIN

½ shallot, finely diced

½ cup crème fraîche or sour cream

½ cup mayonnaise

Finely grated zest of 1 lemon

1 tablespoon freshly squeezed
   lemon juice

1 tablespoon extra-virgin olive oil

1 tablespoon fresh dill, finely chopped

1 to 2 teaspoons wasabi paste or freshly
   grated wasabi

½ teaspoon fine sea salt

1 large English cucumber

1 bunch watercress, picked into
   1-inch sprigs

In a large bowl, whisk together the shallot, crème fraîche, mayonnaise, lemon zest, lemon juice, olive oil, dill, wasabi paste, and salt.

Peel away alternating strips of skin lengthwise on the cucumber, leaving strips of unpeeled skin in between. Cut into ¼-inch rounds. Add the cucumbers to the bowl and toss to combine.

To serve, arrange the watercress on a serving plate and scoop the cucumber salad into the center of the greens. Serve immediately, or refrigerate and serve within 4 hours, scooping onto the watercress just before serving.

GRILLED ASPARAGUS RAFTS
with Sorrel Cream

PINNING ASPARAGUS SPEARS TOGETHER with skewers eliminates the frustration of losing individual spears through the grill grates and makes it easier to cook the asparagus evenly on both sides. Jumbo spears, blanched to soften them, are the best size for skewering. Sorrel greens add that essence of lemon that brings out the best in fresh asparagus. If you forgo the sauce, squeeze fresh lemon juice over the "rafts" just before serving.

SERVES 6 · ACTIVE: 20 MIN · TOTAL: 30 MIN

2 bunches jumbo asparagus
(about 2 pounds)

Fine sea salt

1 tablespoon extra-virgin olive oil

Freshly ground black pepper

½ cup heavy cream

2 cups fresh sorrel leaves, thinly sliced

1 tablespoon chopped fresh chives

Prepare a hot grill and oil the grill rack. Bring a pot of salted water to a boil. Prepare a large bowl of salted ice water.

Snap the stem of one asparagus spear to see where the stem gets tough. Use that as a reference and trim all the spears on a slight bias to the same length. Blanch the spears in the boiling water for 1 minute, then dunk them in ice water for 30 seconds to stop the cooking.

Put 12 (6-inch) bamboo skewers in the hot blanching water for a few minutes to help prevent them from burning on the grill. Meanwhile, drain and dry the asparagus. Lay the spears flat on a cutting board and line up the tips. Remove the skewers from the water.

About 1 inch from the bottom of a spear, push a skewer perpendicular through the center. Pass the skewer through 5 more spears. Repeat this step, pushing another skewer through the 6 spears about 1 inch below their tips. You will end up with a raft of 6 spears connected by skewers at the top and bottom. Continue in this way to make the remaining rafts. Brush each one with the olive oil and season with salt and pepper.

Grill the asparagus rafts until they're slightly charred, about 2 minutes on each side.

Heat the cream in a saucepan over medium-low heat. Add the sorrel, chives, ¼ teaspoon salt, and a few turns of black pepper. Wilt the sorrel leaves in the sauce for about 2 minutes. Spoon the sauce over the asparagus and serve.

ROASTED ASPARAGUS

with Triple Crème Sauce and Tarragon

THE ADVANTAGE OF ROASTING pencil-thin asparagus stalks is that they cook faster, and brown more quickly, than thicker stalks. Here they become crunchy and caramelized, almost like French fries. Add the cheese and make a farm-to-table version of cheese fries. If you prefer a lighter, nondairy alternative, skip the sauce and top the roasted asparagus with Shallot-Herb Pistou (page 19).

SERVES 4 · ACTIVE: 20 MIN · TOTAL: 20 MIN

3 bunches pencil-thin asparagus
(about 3 pounds)

2 tablespoons extra-virgin olive oil

1 teaspoon fine sea salt

2 tablespoons tarragon vinegar

1 shallot, thinly sliced

¼ cup heavy cream

3 ounces triple crème cheese, such as
Saint-André, rind removed, cut into
small cubes

1 tablespoon chopped fresh chives

1 tablespoon chopped fresh tarragon

1 teaspoon finely grated lemon zest

Preheat the oven to 400°F.

Remove the tough ends of the asparagus and compost or discard. In a bowl, toss the asparagus with the olive oil and salt. Heat a large, heavy ovenproof skillet or roasting pan in the oven for 5 minutes. Carefully add the asparagus to the hot skillet. It will sizzle a little from the heat. Give it a stir to evenly distribute the oil and asparagus in the pan. Roast until the asparagus is slightly charred and tender, 8 to 10 minutes, tossing them once halfway through.

While the asparagus roasts, cook the vinegar and shallot in a small saucepan over medium heat until the vinegar has evaporated, about 4 minutes. Add the cream and reduce it by one-quarter, about 3 minutes. Reduce the heat to low and stir in the cheese until it's fully melted. Cook until the sauce is thick enough to coat the asparagus, about 3 minutes more. Stir in the chives, tarragon, and lemon zest. Taste and adjust the seasoning as needed. Drizzle the cheese sauce over the asparagus and serve.

CHILLED ASPARAGUS SOUP

with Egg and Capers

THIS SPRING SOUP IS one of the first things I make when asparagus finally pops out of the ground. The asparagus tips and capers add a crunchy, salty contrast to the silkiness of the soup. If you can get your hands on fresh morels, sauté them with a little garlic and garnish the soup with them.

SERVES 4 TO 6 · ACTIVE: 20 MIN · TOTAL: I HR 30 MIN

Fine sea salt

2 bunches medium asparagus (about 2 pounds)

1 teaspoon extra-virgin olive oil

1 teaspoon chopped capers

1 teaspoon chopped fresh chives

1 hard-boiled duck or large chicken egg, crumbled

2 tablespoons unsalted butter

1 large shallot, thinly sliced

1 small parsnip, peeled and thinly sliced

1 tablespoon dry white wine

3 cups Vegetable Stock (page 292)

Freshly ground black pepper

½ cup plain yogurt

½ cup goat cheese

Bring a pot of salted water to a boil. Prepare a large bowl of salted ice water.

Remove the tough ends of the asparagus and compost or discard. Separate the tips from the stalks. Boil the tips until almost tender, about 2 minutes. Drain and immediately transfer to the bowl of ice water. Drain again and dry the tips.

In a small bowl, combine the asparagus tips, olive oil, capers, chives, and egg. Set aside.

Melt the butter in a medium saucepan over low heat. Add the shallot and cook until translucent, about 3 minutes. Add the parsnip slices, cover, and cook until tender but not brown, about 5 minutes. Add the wine and cook for another 2 to 3 minutes, until the wine is almost completely reduced. Pour in the vegetable stock, 1 teaspoon salt, and two turns of black pepper and bring to a boil. Reduce the heat to medium, add the asparagus stalks, and simmer until just tender, about 10 minutes. Remove the pan from the heat and let cool for 5 minutes.

Transfer the contents of the saucepan to a blender and puree. Pulse in the yogurt and goat cheese until just combined. Taste and adjust the seasoning as needed. Chill for 1 hour. If needed, adjust the consistency by adding a bit more stock; adjust the seasoning again. Serve in chilled bowls with a sprinkling of the asparagus tip mixture over the top.

A Simple Tomato Salad

You don't have to cook fancy or complicated masterpieces—
just good food from fresh ingredients.

JULIA CHILD

Most summer nights at my restaurant, we make one particular dish for almost every table: the tomato salad. It's straightforward, but incredibly satisfying. To make it, I marinate fresh heirloom tomatoes in extra-virgin olive oil, local gin, a bit of sea salt, and fresh herbs.

As uncomplicated as the salad is, it took me years to learn to make it. Its evolution mirrors the way I've changed as a cook: once reveling in complex techniques, now finding joy in simplicity.

The dish originated with an heirloom tomato terrine I made at a four-star restaurant in Manhattan, which involved roasting tomatoes in olive oil for 24 hours, meticulously peeling them and removing their seeds, making a gelatin out of tomato water, layering it all in a terrine mold to set for a day, and making a tomato-gin foam to serve on top. It was a long, technical process that would never fly at a casual Brooklyn restaurant or at home, so I edited out all but the few elements I needed to retain the flavors and balance of the dish.

Surprisingly, the relaxed Brooklyn version of this tomato terrine became the dish that put me on the culinary map in New York. In his review of James, *The New York Times* restaurant critic Frank Bruni wrote, "No bigger, brasher restaurant around town served me an heirloom tomato salad this summer that I enjoyed any more than the one at James."

Even in the biggest, most competitive city, the straightforward nature of a simple tomato salad using the best ingredients and a touch of flair can be a winner. That salad represents an important lesson: Fresh, quality ingredients produce delicious food on their own. Sometimes, your job is to let the ingredients do the work. ❧

HEIRLOOM TOMATOES

with Gin, Feta, and Dill

THIS IS THE BEST way I know to treat ripe heirloom tomatoes at the height of summer. It's simple and stunning, especially if you use a mix of tomato varieties, colors, and sizes. The gin adds depth and brings out the vegetal flavor and scent of the tomatoes. Any high-quality, traditional English gin with a strong juniper aroma will work well.

SERVES 4 TO 6 · ACTIVE: 10 MIN · TOTAL: 40 MIN

2 pounds mixed heirloom tomatoes, stems removed

¼ teaspoon fine sea salt

Freshly ground black pepper

2 tablespoons extra-virgin olive oil (preferably a young, fruity one)

2 teaspoons gin

¼ cup loosely packed coarsely chopped dill

1 large shallot, finely chopped (about 2 tablespoons)

4 ounces sheep's milk feta cheese, crumbled

Core the tomatoes and slice into ¼-inch rounds. Season on both sides with the salt and a few turns of black pepper.

Layer the tomato slices in a large bowl, drizzling the olive oil, gin, and a sprinkle of dill and shallots evenly between each layer. Cover with plastic wrap and let sit at room temperature for 30 minutes, gently tossing after 15 minutes.

Layer the tomatoes on a large serving platter, sprinkling feta evenly between each layer. Whisk the remaining liquid from the first bowl and pour it over the tomatoes. Serve at room temperature.

TOMATO AND GRUYÈRE TART

THIS CLASSIC TOMATO TART is an easy-to-assemble showstopper. Regular beefsteak tomatoes are great here—no need for pricier heirlooms since you're baking them. Once you have this tart down, play around with different herbs and cheeses: Substitute sage for the marjoram and blue cheese for the Gruyère for a stronger flavor, or add a chopped anchovy to the herb-oil mixture before brushing it over the top. Serve the tart warm just after baking it, or make it a day ahead, refrigerate it, and bring it to room temperature before serving.

SERVES 4 TO 6 · ACTIVE: 20 MIN · TOTAL: 2 HR 20 MIN

1 Savory Tart Crust (page 284)

2 tablespoons plus 2 teaspoons extra-virgin olive oil

4 large shallots, thinly sliced

2 tablespoons chopped fresh chives

Fine sea salt and freshly ground black pepper

12 ounces aged Gruyère cheese; 8 ounces sliced, 4 ounces coarsely grated

2 tablespoons smooth Dijon mustard

2 tablespoons coarse-ground mustard

2 pounds ripe large red and yellow tomatoes, stems removed and cut into ¼-inch-thick slices

3 tablespoons chopped fresh marjoram

Preheat the oven to 350°F. Butter and flour a 9 x 13 x 1-inch rectangular tart pan or a 9½-inch round tart pan.

On a lightly floured surface, roll out the dough into a rectangle or circle (depending on the pan you're using) about ⅛ inch thick and a bit bigger than the pan you're using. Transfer the dough to the pan, letting it hang slightly over the edges. Trim off the excess dough and prick holes all over with a fork. Bake until the dough just starts to turn light brown, about 20 minutes. Remove from the oven and let cool for a few minutes.

In a large sauté pan over medium-low heat, heat 2 teaspoons of the olive oil and cook the shallots until they're soft and translucent, about 10 minutes. Stir in the chives, a large pinch of salt, and four turns of black pepper and remove from the heat.

Evenly layer the sliced cheese to cover the bottom of the tart dough. Spread both mustards over the cheese and evenly distribute the shallots on top of the mustard. Finally, layer the sliced tomatoes by alternating a row of red tomatoes with a row of yellow tomatoes, overlapping each slice by about ½ inch. If using a round pan, start from the outside, working in. Bake until the crust is golden brown and the tomatoes are soft, about 40 minutes.

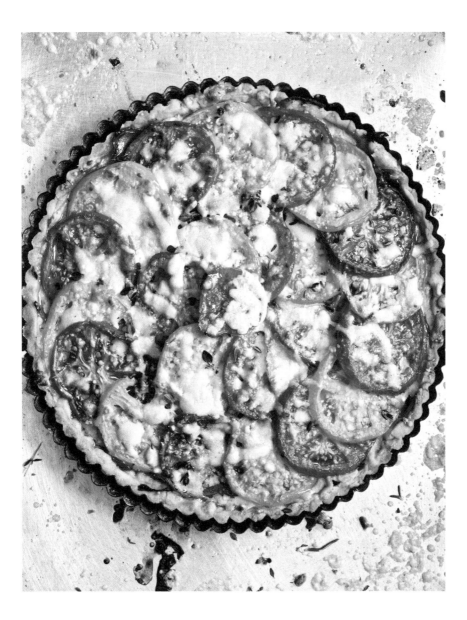

Combine the remaining 2 tablespoons olive oil with the marjoram and a pinch of salt. Gently brush the marjoram mixture on the tomatoes with a pastry brush. Sprinkle the grated cheese evenly over the tomatoes. Bake for another 20 minutes or so, until the crust is a nice golden brown, the cheese on top is melted, and the tomatoes are soft. Let cool for 10 to 15 minutes before serving.

TOMATO AND MUSTARD RELISH

AS A YOUNG COOK in Boston, I made this relish for staff meal, and the head chef liked it so much she turned it into a sauce for filet mignon and added it to the menu. It's as delicious piled on grilled hot dogs and hamburgers as it is gilding a fancy steak. Wherever ketchup and mustard go, this relish has a place. I prefer it at room temperature, but it works cold or warm, too.

MAKES ABOUT 1 CUP · ACTIVE: 20 MIN · TOTAL: 40 MIN

2 tablespoons unsalted butter

1 small shallot, finely chopped (2 to 3 tablespoons)

1 teaspoon mirin

1 teaspoon white wine vinegar

1 teaspoon soy sauce or tamari

4 ripe plum tomatoes, peeled, seeded, and cut into ¼-inch dice

1 tablespoon whole-grain mustard

1 teaspoon Roasted Garlic Puree (page 77), or ½ teaspoon finely grated garlic

1 teaspoon chopped fresh thyme leaves

1 tablespoon sliced fresh flat-leaf parsley

Freshly ground black pepper

A few drops of wasabi oil

Melt the butter in a sauté pan over medium heat. Add the shallot and cook until translucent with no browning, about 3 minutes. (If using fresh garlic instead of puree, add it with the shallots.) Add the mirin, vinegar, and soy sauce. Cook for 1 minute, then add the tomatoes, mustard, and garlic puree. Increase the heat to medium-high and continue cooking until most of the moisture is evaporated and the mixture has thickened to a relish-like consistency, about 5 minutes. Add the thyme and remove from the heat. Stir in the parsley, two turns of black pepper, and the wasabi oil. Taste and adjust the seasoning as needed. Refrigerate in an airtight container for up to 2 days.

MELTED CHERRY TOMATOES

with Sweet Marjoram

GOOD THINGS HAPPEN WHEN tomatoes are roasted in a bath of olive oil: As their skins pop, their juices mingle with the oil, shallots, and garlic, and become a delicious mess. You can serve this as a side dish or store it in a jar for a few weeks in the fridge. Dress up plain pasta, spread it on a sandwich, or spoon it over fish—you'll find a million ways to use this once you have it on hand.

SERVES 4 · ACTIVE: 10 MIN · TOTAL: 40 MIN

¼ cup extra-virgin olive oil

4 pints mixed cherry and golden
tomatoes, stems removed

¼ teaspoon fine sea salt

1 large shallot, finely chopped
(about 3 tablespoons)

1 garlic clove, finely chopped
(about 1 teaspoon)

2 marjoram sprigs, leaves removed and
coarsely chopped (fresh oregano or
rosemary also works)

⅛ teaspoon freshly ground black pepper

Preheat the oven to 400°F.

Pour the olive oil into a heavy 2-quart casserole dish and put it in the oven for about 5 minutes. When the pan is hot, but not smoking, carefully add the tomatoes and toss to coat them in the oil. Roast the tomatoes until they burst, about 10 minutes.

Add the salt, shallot, and garlic to the casserole dish and stir to combine with the tomatoes. Roast until the shallots are translucent and the tomatoes are soft and broken up, about 20 minutes.

Stir in the marjoram and pepper and let sit for a few minutes to allow the herb to infuse the dish. Just before serving, carefully pour the liquid in the pan into a serving bowl and whisk to create a rich, thick tomato vinaigrette. Add the tomatoes to the serving bowl and toss to coat them in the liquid.

BABY KALE AND QUINOA SALAD

with Almonds, Roasted Garlic, and Poached Eggs

YEARS AGO, MY BUSINESS partner, Deborah, suggested we add a kale salad to the menu at James. I wasn't so hot on the idea, but she assured me kale would be huge. This is now one of our most popular dishes, and has enough richness to stand alone as a light main course.

SERVES 4 · ACTIVE: 20 MIN · TOTAL: 45 MIN

For the almonds:

½ teaspoon extra-virgin olive oil

¼ teaspoon smoked paprika

Fine sea salt

½ cup whole raw almonds, skin-on

For the quinoa:

Fine sea salt

⅓ cup red or black quinoa

2 tablespoons sliced fresh flat-leaf parsley

1 teaspoon finely grated lemon zest

1 teaspoon freshly squeezed lemon juice

2 teaspoons extra-virgin olive oil

For the kale salad:

2 tablespoons Roasted Garlic Puree (page 77)

1 teaspoon smooth Dijon mustard

1 tablespoon plus 1 teaspoon red wine vinegar

2 tablespoons extra-virgin olive oil

2 tablespoons avocado oil

8 ounces baby kale

½ cup grated ricotta salata or Parmigiano-Reggiano

Fine sea salt and freshly ground black pepper

4 eggs, soft poached (see page 196)

To make the almonds, preheat the oven to 350°F. In a bowl, combine the oil, smoked paprika, and a pinch of salt. Toss the almonds in the seasoned oil, transfer them to a baking sheet and roast for 10 minutes, shaking the pan once halfway through cooking.

To make the quinoa, bring 6 cups salted water to a boil. Add the quinoa and simmer until tender, about 15 minutes, then drain and cool. Stir in a pinch of salt, the parsley, lemon zest, lemon juice, and olive oil. Reserve at room temperature.

To make the kale salad: In a large bowl, whisk together the garlic puree and mustard until smooth. Add the vinegar and slowly pour in the olive and avocado oils in a steady stream, whisking constantly until well combined. Add the kale, roasted almonds, cheese, and cooked quinoa to the vinaigrette, and gently toss. Season with salt and pepper to taste. Divide the salad among four bowls, and top each serving with a poached egg.

KALE AND RICOTTA PANISSE

THE FRIED CHICKPEA FLOUR cakes called *panisse* in the south of France aren't well known in America, which is surprising: they're gluten-free and easy to make. Making *panisse* batter is similar to making polenta, but quicker because chickpea flour is so fine.

SERVES 4 TO 6 · ACTIVE: 20 MIN · TOTAL: 50 MIN

About ½ cup extra-virgin olive oil

1 large bunch lacinato kale, stems trimmed and cut into ¼-inch pieces (about 4 cups)

2 teaspoons minced garlic

Fine sea salt and freshly ground black pepper

2 cups Vegetable Stock (page 292) or water

1 cup chickpea flour

3 cups fresh ricotta cheese, plus more for serving (optional)

1 lemon, cut into 4 to 6 wedges

Coat a 6 x 9-inch baking dish with olive oil.

Heat 2 tablespoons of the olive oil in a large sauté pan over medium-high heat. Add the kale, garlic, ¼ teaspoon salt, and a few turns of black pepper. Reduce the heat to medium and cook until the kale is wilted and tender, about 5 minutes. If the kale is still tough, add a few tablespoons of water and cook until the water evaporates. Taste and adjust the seasoning and set aside.

In a large pot, bring the vegetable stock, 2 teaspoons of the olive oil, and ¼ teaspoon salt to a boil. Reduce the heat to medium-low and gradually pour in the chickpea flour, whisking until smooth. Reduce the heat to low and cook, stirring frequently, until it's very thick, about 10 minutes. Stir in the kale, remove the pot from the heat, and let it cool for 2 to 3 minutes. Add the cheese and stir until well combined. Taste and adjust the seasoning.

Pour the batter into the greased baking dish and spread it into an even layer. Let cool at room temperature until the *panisse* sets, 20 to 30 minutes. It should pull away from the sides of the dish a bit. Transfer the *panisse* onto a cutting board by turning over the baking dish. Cut into 2- to 3-inch squares.

In a large sauté pan over medium heat, heat ¼ cup of the olive oil. When the oil is hot, add half of the *panisse* squares and brown on both sides, 3 to 5 minutes per side. Transfer to paper towels to drain any excess oil. Repeat with the remaining squares. Serve hot with a dollop of fresh ricotta, a drizzle of olive oil, and a squeeze of fresh lemon juice.

BLACK KALE AND CABBAGE SALAD

ONE OF MY EARLIEST cooking jobs called for making batches upon batches of cold sesame noodles at a gourmet food shop. The dressing, with tamari, ginger, and sesame oil, is what made it so good, so I started using it in salads. You can serve this right away, but I find it's best after a few hours in the fridge—the raw kale softens a bit and soaks up the flavors. It's a simple way to turn reluctant kale eaters on to this amazing green.

SERVES 4 TO 6 · ACTIVE: 30 MIN · TOTAL: 30 MIN

½ cup white sesame seeds

1 bunch lacinato kale (about 1 pound)

1 small head red cabbage (about 1 pound)

1-inch piece fresh ginger, peeled and chopped

5 tablespoons extra-virgin olive oil

¼ cup toasted sesame oil

3 tablespoons rice vinegar

3 tablespoons tamari or soy sauce

1 tablespoon mirin or honey

Preheat the oven to 350°F.

Toast the sesame seeds on a baking sheet in the oven until golden brown, about 15 minutes, tossing them once halfway through.

Meanwhile, remove the ribs and stems from the kale. Ribbon-cut the kale leaves (see page 17) and finely chop the stems and ribs. Quarter the cabbage and compost or discard the core. Slice the cabbage into ¼-inch strips.

In a blender, blend half of the toasted sesame seeds until finely ground. Add the ginger, olive oil, sesame oil, vinegar, tamari, and mirin and blend until well combined, about 2 minutes. Toss the kale, cabbage, dressing, and the remaining sesame seeds together in a large serving bowl.

CORN BROTH

THIS SILKY BROTH IS rich, sweet, and versatile. In the summer, when locally grown sweet corn is abundant, I use it as the base for a variety of dishes. It holds its own as a simple, refreshing soup but can also be used for risotto, chowder, and the corn and oyster soup on page 64. If the corn you use is very sweet, finish the broth with a tablespoon of white wine vinegar to balance it out.

MAKES 2 QUARTS · ACTIVE: 15 MINUTES · TOTAL: 1 HR

6 ears fresh sweet corn, shucked, kernels removed, cobs reserved

1 teaspoon coriander seeds

1 cup dry white wine

1 teaspoon whole white peppercorns

½ teaspoon fine sea salt

1 fresh bay leaf

1 lemon thyme sprig (regular thyme works too)

1 onion, cut into medium dice

2 garlic cloves, crushed

1 tablespoon fine corn flour (all-purpose flour is a good substitute)

4 tablespoons unsalted butter

Cut the cobs into short chunks using a cleaver or heavy knife.

In a medium pot over medium heat, lightly toast the coriander seeds until they just start to smoke. Add the cobs, wine, 8 cups water, peppercorns, salt, bay leaf, thyme, onion, and garlic. Reduce the heat to low and simmer for 45 minutes.

Pour the broth into a fine-mesh strainer set over a large bowl, reserving the liquid. Discard the solids. Return the corn broth to the pot and bring to a simmer. Add the corn kernels and cook until tender, about 5 minutes.

In a blender, puree the broth with the flour and butter until it becomes a smooth puree, the consistency of a light tomato sauce (you may have to puree the broth in batches). Use immediately, or let cool to room temperature and refrigerate in an airtight container for up to 5 days, or freeze for up to 3 months.

CORN SOUP

with Oysters, Pickled Corn, and Tarragon

MONTAUK, THE FAR EASTERN end of Long Island, is one of my favorite places to enjoy the summer. Surrounded by some of the best oysters and a bounty of fresh corn, I inevitably put the two together and make this soup every time I'm there. It's reminiscent of chowder, but much lighter, and the pickled corn adds bright, crunchy contrast. Tarragon vinegar is easier to find than you might think, but you can make your own by adding a few sprigs of fresh tarragon to a bottle of white wine or champagne vinegar and letting it sit for a few days (see Preserving Herbs, page 18).

SERVES 4 TO 6 · ACTIVE: 20 MIN · TOTAL: 45 MIN

Fine sea salt	2 tablespoons tarragon vinegar
1 cup fresh corn kernels	1 tablespoon extra-virgin olive oil
1 small shallot, finely diced	2 quarts Corn Broth (page 63)
Freshly ground black pepper	1 cup coarse cornmeal
2 teaspoons sliced fresh tarragon	2 tablespoons vegetable oil
2 teaspoons sliced fresh chives or scallions	8 to 12 freshly shucked oysters (plan on 2 per serving)

Bring a medium pot of salted water to a boil. Add the corn kernels, cook for 1 minute, and drain.

In a medium bowl, combine the corn kernels, shallot, two turns of black pepper, ¼ teaspoon salt, the tarragon, chives, vinegar, and olive oil. Let sit at room temperature for about 30 minutes.

In a medium pot, bring the corn broth to a simmer over medium heat. Taste and adjust the seasoning if necessary.

Mix together the cornmeal and a pinch of salt in a bowl. Heat the vegetable oil in a large sauté pan over medium heat. Dredge the oysters in the cornmeal until well coated. Gently add the oysters to the hot oil and fry until light golden brown, about 2 minutes on each side. Transfer the oysters to a paper towel–lined plate to remove any excess oil.

Ladle the hot corn broth into warm bowls. Float 2 oysters in the center of each bowl and drizzle the pickled corn around the oysters. Serve immediately.

Appalachia in a Four-Star Restaurant

The pleasures of the rustic and urban lifestyles
are essentially the same.

There may be no other vegetable whose arrival at the farmers' market causes as much of a frenzy as ramps. One of the first greens of spring, these peppery, pungent onions are found only in the wild and are in season only for a hot minute.

Their current popularity among high-end chefs is mind-blowing when you consider that ramps have the most modest of origins in Appalachia. In fact, I first learned of ramps while hiking south on the Appalachian Trail, where beds and beds of vibrant green shoots blanketed the woods. Back then, they weren't the darlings of the farmers' markets. I had a few years of cooking under my belt, but I had never heard of ramps, much less tasted one.

Those ramps were a welcome addition to the instant macaroni and cheese I lived on that spring. I was ravenous from burning so many calories carrying my pack. While I trudged through the forest, I daydreamed about ingredients, creating imaginary menus and tasting each dish the way a dehydrated castaway hallucinates about a drink.

Ramps are fleeting—up for grabs for only a few short weeks at the start of spring, so those who live along the trail have a tradition of stockpiling, pickling, and preserving ramps for the months ahead. The locals were harvesting bags and bags of ramps for their personal use.

I was fortunate to meet a local guy camping out who fed me a stew of ramps, wild potatoes, and venison. It was a real backwoods scene, with a giant, steaming iron cauldron simmering over the red-hot coals of an open fire. The stew was delicious. Rejuvenating. Ethereal, even. Was it delicious because I was so hungry? Was it the beauty of my surroundings? It was a truly memorable experience, and I figured that once I left the mountains I would never see ramps again nor taste anything like that stew.

Back in New York, worlds away, I landed a gig at the original Bouley restaurant in Tribeca. On my second day of work, I was instructed to clean and blanch the delicate leaves of wild leeks, as the French sous-chef called them, and carefully wrap them around tiny loins of lamb. The intricate tediousness of the task intimidated me. Then, as I grabbed the boxes full of wild leeks, a familiar scent swirled around me and I laughed out loud. The wild leeks were the same ramps that the rustic Appalachian folks treasured so much. The fancy dish was just a trumped-up version of that rural stew.

Quality ingredients and flavor combinations transcend geographic and cultural boundaries. They straddle simplicity and sophistication. The pleasures that make the rustic and urban lifestyles enjoyable are one and the same; they are just dressed up a little differently. ❧

ROASTED CORN AND DUCK CONFIT SALAD

ON ITS OWN OR as a side to roasted or grilled meat or fish, this easy salad is a way to turn corn into a substantial dish. Duck confit adds savory richness to corn's sweetness. If you've already got the grill going, husk the corn, brush it with olive oil, and grill it instead of toasting it in the pan.

SERVES 4 TO 6 · ACTIVE: 30 MIN · TOTAL: 30 MIN

2 tablespoons extra-virgin olive oil

3 ears corn, shucked and kernels removed

Fine sea salt and freshly ground black pepper

8 ounces frisée, stems removed and coarsely chopped

1 pint red and yellow cherry tomatoes, halved

4 legs duck confit, shredded

1 tablespoon chopped fresh sweet marjoram

1 tablespoon sliced fresh flat-leaf parsley

1 tablespoon chopped fresh chives

¼ cup Sherry-Shallot Vinaigrette (page 286)

Heat the olive oil in a large sauté pan over medium-high heat. Add the corn kernels and cook, tossing constantly, until the corn browns and pops. Season with salt and pepper to taste. Transfer to a large bowl and toss with the frisée, tomatoes, duck confit, marjoram, parsley, chives, and vinaigrette. Season with salt and pepper to taste, and serve.

SPRING ONION SOUP

with Pecorino and Bacon

SPRING ONIONS RESEMBLE SCALLIONS but generally have fatter bulbs and a brighter, sweeter flavor. Here, their oniony perfume is boosted by a sprinkle of salty cheese and the smokiness of bacon. Be sure not to cook the soup any longer than necessary because you want to preserve that heady spring onion aroma that makes the soup so enticing.

SERVES 4 · ACTIVE: 20 MIN · TOTAL: 30 MIN

5 medium spring onions
   with greens

2 ramps

2 cups spinach

6 tablespoons unsalted butter

Fine sea salt

½ cup dry white wine

2 quarts Vegetable Stock (page 292)
   or water

1 teaspoon finely grated lemon zest

Freshly ground black pepper

½ cup freshly grated Pecorino Romano

4 slices bacon, preferably a heritage
   breed, cooked and crumbled

Preheat the oven to 350°F.

Cut and reserve the green tops from the bulbs of the spring onions and ramps. Trim the roots and remove the outer layer of the bulbs. Thoroughly rinse the trimmed bulbs in cold water to remove any dirt. Cut the spring onion bulbs and ramp bulbs into ¼-inch-thick slices. Coarsely chop the spinach and the reserved greens from the onions and ramps.

Melt the butter in a 4-quart saucepan over low heat. Add the sliced ramp and onion bulbs and a pinch of salt. Cook until the onions are translucent and tender, about 10 minutes, stirring occasionally. Add the chopped onion greens and ramp greens and continue cooking until they're tender, about 5 minutes.

Add the wine and cook for about 2 minutes. Pour in the vegetable stock and bring to a gentle simmer. Cook the greens for about 10 minutes. Add the spinach and cook for 2 minutes to wilt.

Working in batches if necessary, fill half the blender with equal parts liquid and greens. Starting on low speed and gradually increasing to high, blend until smooth. Transfer to another pot over low heat, stir in the lemon zest, and adjust the consistency with vegetable stock or water. Season with salt and pepper to taste. Serve in warm soup bowls with a sprinkle of grated cheese and bacon pieces.

CIPOLLINI ONION BRÛLÉE

with Balsamic Vinegar and Rosemary

BRÛLÉE MEANS "BURNED," WHICH is exactly what you're going for here. Cipollinis are mild and sweet and taste even better once they're charred. Try this on crostini with sharp cheese, serve with grilled and roasted meats, or top your hamburger with a generous scoop.

MAKES 1 QUART · ACTIVE: 25 MIN · TOTAL: 35 MIN

1 pound cipollini onions, peeled and halved through the core

¼ teaspoon fine sea salt

1 tablespoon extra-virgin olive oil

¼ cup balsamic vinegar

1 tablespoon finely chopped fresh rosemary or 1 teaspoon dried rosemary

Freshly ground black pepper

In a bowl, toss the onions with the salt.

In a large sauté pan over high heat, heat the oil until it starts to quiver. Arrange the onions cut side down in the pan in one layer. (If they don't all fit in one layer, cook in two batches, adding a touch of oil between batches.) Cook without moving until the cut sides of the onions are black and charred, 3 to 5 minutes.

When all the onions are blackened on the cut side, place them all back in the pan (if you cooked in batches) and toss with the vinegar and rosemary. Cook until the balsamic vinegar is almost dry and coats the onions, 2 to 4 minutes. The onions should be cooked through, but not meltingly soft. Add four turns of black pepper and taste and adjust the salt, if needed. Serve immediately, or let cool and refrigerate in an airtight container for up to 1 week.

LEEK CONFIT

LEEK CONFIT IS ONE of those condiments you'll find a million uses for once you have it around. Its satiny texture and subdued onion flavor are at home just about anywhere you would put sautéed onions: tucked into an omelet, spread on crostini with goat cheese, or tossed into pasta dishes or with roasted vegetables. I also serve this as a simple side dish with roasted chicken. For extra richness, grate some Parmigiano-Reggiano or Gruyère cheese over the warm leeks, and add a sprinkle of fresh herbs. The ideal leeks have long, firm, mostly white stems—the green parts aren't as tender or flavorful.

MAKES ABOUT 1 QUART · ACTIVE: 15 MIN · TOTAL: 1 HR

2 pounds leeks, white and pale green parts only, ends trimmed

⅛ teaspoon fine sea salt

1½ cups Vegetable Stock (page 292) or water

½ cup dry white wine

¼ cup extra-virgin olive oil

1 thyme sprig, cut into 1-inch pieces

1 fresh bay leaf

1-inch piece orange peel

1 teaspoon whole black peppercorns

Preheat the oven to 325°F.

Remove the tough outer layer of each leek. Rinse the leeks, paying special attention to where the pale green and white parts meet.

Arrange the leeks in one layer in a baking dish, cutting them to fit if necessary. Sprinkle with the salt and cover with the vegetable stock, wine, and olive oil.

Make a spice pouch by placing the thyme, bay leaf, orange peel, and peppercorns on a 12-inch square of cheesecloth. Fold in the corners to create a loose pouch and tie together with a piece of kitchen twine. Submerge the pouch in the cooking liquid.

Cover the dish with aluminum foil and bake for 1 hour. The leeks should be soft and tender, giving little resistance when pierced with a cake tester or sharp paring knife.

Store the leeks, with the cooking liquid from the dish (discard the spice pouch), in an airtight container in the refrigerator for up to 1 week.

VENISON AND RAMP STEW

IN EARLY SPRING, THE most coveted vegetable at the farmers' market is the ramp. There's good reason for the mad scramble to get them—not only do ramps have a fleeting season, but they also have a fantastically pungent, garlicky flavor. They're especially well suited to the bold flavors of lamb and venison and add sharpness to this hearty, warming stew. Venison is becoming easier to find, but if you can't get your hands on it, beef or lamb stew meat would also be delicious.

SERVES 4 TO 6 · ACTIVE: 30 MIN · TOTAL: 2 HR

2 tablespoons cooking oil

2 pounds venison stew meat, cut into 1-inch pieces

2 tablespoons all-purpose flour

Fine sea salt

24 ramps, greens and bulbs separated and sliced

1 cup baby carrots, mixed colors and sizes, cut into 1-inch pieces

1 cup mixed radishes cut into ½-inch pieces

1 cup baby potatoes (like red bliss or fingerlings)

1 cup red wine

2 cups chopped tomatoes

12 dried juniper berries

2 thyme sprigs

4 flat-leaf parsley sprigs

Freshly ground black pepper

Position a rack in the center of the oven and preheat the oven to 325°F.

Heat the oil in a large Dutch oven over medium heat. Dry the venison with paper towels and toss in a bowl with the flour and a large pinch of salt. Shake off any excess flour and sear the meat in the oil until lightly brown on all sides, about 5 minutes. Transfer to a plate.

Reduce the heat to low and add the ramp bulbs, carrots, radishes, and potatoes. Throw in a pinch of salt. Cook for about 5 minutes, stirring occasionally, until the ramps start to brown. Add the wine and reduce by half. Add the tomatoes, venison, 4 cups water, juniper, thyme, and parsley.

Cover with the lid slightly ajar to let steam out and place on the middle rack in the oven. Cook for 1 hour and 30 minutes, stirring about every 20 minutes.

Add the ramp greens, return to the oven, and cook uncovered for 10 minutes more. The meat and vegetables should be tender and the liquid should be fairly thick and a rich, reddish brown color. Taste and adjust the seasoning as needed.

ROASTED GARLIC PUREE

I USE THIS WHEREVER you might use minced raw garlic: salad dressings, pasta, sauces. It's not as sharp as raw garlic and adds a deeply mellow garlic flavor, so it also works as a condiment for toast, roasted meats, or baked potatoes. The freshest heads of garlic are firm and tight.

MAKES ABOUT ½ CUP · ACTIVE: 15 MIN · TOTAL: 1 HR 15 MIN

4 heads garlic
Extra-virgin olive oil

Fine sea salt

Position a rack in the center of the oven and preheat the oven to 350°F.

Slice one-third off the top of each head of garlic to expose the cloves. (Reserve the scraps for other recipes.) Pour 3 tablespoons olive oil into a small roasting pan and place the garlic cut side down in the oil. Cover the pan with aluminum foil and place on the middle rack. Roast until the garlic is lightly browned and the bulbs are soft, about 1 hour. Set aside until the garlic is cool enough to handle.

Working over a bowl, squeeze the heads of roasted garlic until the cloves fall out. In a blender or food processor, puree the cloves with 2 tablespoons olive oil, 2 tablespoons water, and a pinch of salt until smooth. Transfer the garlic puree to an airtight jar and cover the top with a thin layer of olive oil to help preserve it. Store in the refrigerator for up to 2 weeks, or freeze for up to 3 months.

THREE LEGUME CROSTINIS

THIS IS MY FAVORITE way of eating fresh beans and peas. Shelling fresh beans takes a little extra time, but for making just a couple of cups of puree, the difference in flavor is well worth the effort. Made with fresh beans and peas, the various toppings that follow are creamier and less starchy than canned or dried beans. If you want a gluten-free alternative to bread, spoon the toppings into Belgian endive leaves or on top of halved cherry tomatoes.

MAKES ABOUT 24 CROSTINI · ACTIVE: 5 MIN · TOTAL: 15 MIN

1 baguette

¼ cup extra-virgin olive oil

2 tablespoons fresh thyme leaves

2 garlic cloves, crushed

Fine sea salt and freshly ground black pepper

Cut the baguette on the diagonal into ¼-inch-thick slices. Toss the bread in a bowl with the olive oil and thyme until lightly coated. Add the garlic to the bowl and toss again. Cover tightly with plastic wrap, and let it sit at room temperature for a few hours or up to overnight.

Preheat the oven to 350°F. Discard the garlic and season the sliced bread with salt and pepper to taste. Arrange the slices on a baking sheet and toast in the oven until light brown, about 10 minutes. (Or, grill them on a hot grill until golden brown and slightly charred, 1 to 2 minutes). Store in an airtight container for up to 2 days.

SPRING PEA AND TRUFFLE

Fine sea salt

1½ cups shelled English peas (about 1 pound in the shell)

2 tablespoons freshly grated Parmigiano-Reggiano

1 tablespoon unsalted butter, softened

2 teaspoons finely sliced fresh chives

1 tablespoon white truffle oil

1 cup pea shoots

Bring a pot of salted water to a boil. Blanch the peas in the boiling water until tender but still firm, 3 minutes. Drain and rinse in cold water for 30 seconds to cool them. Chop the peas into small pieces. Combine the peas, cheese, butter, and chives in a bowl and smash together until combined but still chunky. Stir in the truffle oil. Spread on the toasted crostini and garnish with the pea shoots.

{ RECIPE CONTINUES }

CRANBERRY BEAN

Fine sea salt

1 cup shelled fresh cranberry beans
(about 1 pound in the shell)

2 teaspoons freshly squeezed lemon juice

1 tablespoon Roasted Garlic Puree
(page 77) or 1 small garlic clove,
finely chopped

1 teaspoon chopped fresh rosemary

Freshly ground black pepper

½ cup extra-virgin olive oil

Bring a pot of salted water to a boil. Cook the beans in the boiling water until tender, about 20 minutes. Drain well and puree in a food processor with the lemon juice, garlic puree, rosemary, ½ teaspoon salt, and four turns of black pepper. On low speed, pour in the olive oil in a slow, steady stream until combined. Taste and adjust the seasoning if necessary, and spread on the toasted crostini.

FAVA BEAN AND TOMATO

Fine sea salt

1 cup shelled fresh fava beans
(about 1 pound in the shell)

1 cup diced plum tomatoes, seeds
and stems removed

1 tablespoon finely chopped shallot

1 teaspoon rice vinegar

2 teaspoons finely sliced fresh
flat-leaf parsley

2 teaspoons sliced fresh dill

½ teaspoon coarse sea salt

Freshly ground black pepper

Bring a pot of salted water to a boil. Blanch the beans in the boiling water until tender but still firm, 1 minute. Drain and rinse in cold water for 30 seconds to cool them. Peel off and compost or discard the outer skins. Coarsely chop the favas and toss them in a bowl with the tomatoes, shallot, vinegar, parsley, dill, coarse salt, and a couple of turns of black pepper. Pile on the toasted crostini.

SUMMER BEANS

with Bagna Cauda

THIS SALAD IS BEST with a variety of beans—green beans, yellow or purple wax beans, runner beans. The mixed beans and garlicky jab of *bagna cauda*, an Italian dip that works as a dressing, make this salad a bold and colorful side dish for barbecues. Summer beans should snap when you break them (hence their other name, snap beans) and have moist flesh. They all have slightly different cooking times, so take the extra step of blanching them separately.

SERVES 4 TO 6 · ACTIVE: 30 MIN · TOTAL: 30 MIN

Fine sea salt

1 pound mixed fresh summer beans,
    stems trimmed

¼ cup Roasted Garlic Puree (page 77) or
    4 garlic cloves, peeled

1 oil-packed anchovy fillet

½ cup coarsely chopped fresh flat-leaf
    parsley with stems

2 tablespoons fresh oregano leaves

2 tablespoons fresh marjoram leaves

½ teaspoon red pepper flakes

½ cup fruity extra-virgin olive oil

Freshly ground black pepper

Juice of ½ lemon

Bring a large pot three-quarters full of salted water to a boil. Meanwhile, prepare a big bowl with ice water. Once the water boils, blanch each type of bean individually until just shy of tender, removing them with tongs and transferring them to the bowl of ice water to stop the cooking. Remove the beans from the ice water when cooled, drain well, and pat them dry.

Chill the blender container in the freezer for 5 minutes. Add the garlic puree, anchovy, parsley, oregano, marjoram, red pepper flakes, and olive oil to the chilled blender and blend on low speed until the mixture is roughly combined, about 1 minute. Season with salt and pepper to taste. In a large serving bowl, toss the beans with the lemon juice and the *bagna cauda* until well coated. Serve at room temperature.

CRISPY CHICKPEAS

with Rosemary

WE SERVE THESE AS a bar snack at James, and our regulars demanded the recipe be in this book. I'm happy to oblige—they're easy to make and easy to snack on, especially with a good cocktail.

SERVES 4 AS A SNACK · ACTIVE: 10 MIN · TOTAL: 30 MIN

1½ cups cooked chickpeas or 1 (15-ounce) can chickpeas, rinsed, drained, and dried

¼ teaspoon fine sea salt

3 tablespoons extra-virgin olive oil

4 rosemary sprigs, leaves removed and finely chopped

1 tablespoon sliced fresh chives

Finely grated zest of 1 lemon

Freshly ground black pepper

Preheat the oven to 400°F.

Place a large cast-iron skillet in the oven and heat for 5 minutes. In a bowl, toss the chickpeas with the salt and olive oil. Pour the chickpeas into the skillet. Roast for 15 minutes, stirring every 5 minutes, until golden brown and crunchy. Stir in the rosemary and bake until you can smell the rosemary, about 3 minutes. Remove from the oven and toss in the chives, lemon zest, and four turns of black pepper. Serve warm.

GRILLED EGGPLANT

with Merguez and Spearmint

I PREFER JAPANESE EGGPLANTS, which are smaller than the Italian globe variety and have fewer seeds and milder, sweeter flesh. Grill over natural hardwood charcoal. It gets hotter, adds a cleaner smoky flavor, and is free of synthetic chemicals.

SERVES 4 TO 6 · ACTIVE: 20 MIN · TOTAL: 20 MIN

6 Italian or Japanese eggplants, cut into ¾-inch-thick disks

3 tablespoons extra-virgin olive oil

1 tablespoon ground coriander

½ teaspoon fine sea salt

1 pound merguez lamb sausage

2 tablespoons Sherry-Shallot Vinaigrette (page 286)

¼ cup fresh spearmint leaves, coarsely chopped

2 tablespoons fresh cilantro leaves, coarsely chopped

Prepare a hot grill and oil the grill rack.

In a bowl, combine the eggplant, olive oil, coriander, and salt, and toss so the eggplant absorbs all the oil.

Grill the sausage until firm and the internal temperature is 145°F, about 10 minutes total, turning it once after about 5 minutes. Grill the eggplant slices until they're soft in the center, about 2 minutes per side.

Cut the sausage and eggplant into 1-inch pieces and toss in a serving bowl with the eggplant and vinaigrette. Just before serving, add the spearmint and cilantro and toss to combine.

EGGPLANT FRIES

with Curry Aioli

I'VE INCLUDED DEEP-FRYING AND baking methods here, so you can choose how indulgent you want to go. Either way, the fries will be crispy and golden on the outside, with meltingly soft, airy centers. Dipped in creamy curry aioli, these fries are a good example of taking a familiar dish like French fries to a whole different level by using a few commonly available alternative ingredients.

SERVES 4 · ACTIVE: 20 MIN · TOTAL: 30 MIN

1 medium eggplant (about 1 pound)

1 large egg

⅓ cup all-purpose flour

Fine sea salt and freshly ground black pepper

1 cup bread crumbs, preferably panko (Japanese-style bread crumbs)

½ teaspoon ground coriander

1 cup safflower oil (if deep-frying) or 2 tablespoons vegetable oil (if baking)

Curry Aioli (page 88)

Peel the eggplant and cut it into strips the size of steak fries, about 1 inch thick and 3 inches long.

Whisk the egg in a large bowl. In another bowl, combine the flour with ¼ teaspoon of salt and a few turns of black pepper. In a third bowl, toss the bread crumbs with the coriander and a pinch of salt. Dredge each eggplant fry in the seasoned flour and shake off any excess. Then dip them in the egg, and coat with the bread crumb mixture.

For deep frying: In a large skillet, heat the frying oil to 325°F. Fry the eggplant strips until golden brown, about 3 minutes on each side. Drain them on a paper towel–lined plate, and season with salt and pepper.

For baking: Preheat the oven to 350°F. Place a skillet or heavy roasting pan with the vegetable oil in the oven for about 5 minutes. To make sure the oil is hot enough, drop one eggplant strip into the oil—it should sizzle a bit. Arrange the eggplant fries in one layer with a least ½ inch between the pieces. Bake for 10 minutes, then flip them over and bake until golden brown, about another 10 minutes. Drain the fries on a paper towel–lined plate or a baking rack with a sheet pan underneath. Season with salt and pepper.

Serve the eggplant fries with curry aioli.

CURRY AIOLI

MAKES 1½ CUPS

1 large egg

1 small garlic clove, peeled

2 tablespoons freshly squeezed lime juice
    (lemon juice is good too)

2 tablespoons mild curry powder

½ teaspoon fine sea salt

¼ cup extra-virgin olive oil

½ cup vegetable oil

¼ cup sour cream or crème fraîche

Freshly ground black pepper

Fresh cilantro leaves, for garnish

Put the egg, garlic, lime juice, curry powder, and salt in a blender and, with the blender running on low speed, pour in the olive oil in a slow, steady stream until combined. With the blender off, scrape down the sides with a rubber spatula. On low speed again, stream in the vegetable oil until the mixture comes to a mayonnaise-like consistency. Transfer the aioli to a bowl and whisk in the sour cream and two turns of black pepper. Taste and adjust the seasoning, if necessary, and garnish with cilantro leaves.

SMOKY EGGPLANT PUREE

with Roasted Broccoli and Ricotta Salata

COOKING EGGPLANT WHOLE OVER a flame results in smoky, silky flesh that becomes a sauce for crunchy, roasted broccoli florets. Perked up with the heat of red pepper flakes and the saltiness of ricotta salata, this salad is a delicious mash-up of contrasting textures and flavors.

ACTIVE: 15 MIN · TOTAL: 40 MIN

2 small eggplants

2 heads broccoli, cut into 1-inch florets

¼ cup extra-virgin olive oil

¾ teaspoon fine sea salt

Finely grated zest and juice of 1 lemon

Pinch of red pepper flakes

1 tablespoon fresh marjoram leaves

1 cup grated ricotta salata

Preheat the oven to 375°F.

Cook the whole eggplants over a gas burner with a medium flame, turning frequently, until they are completely soft and collapsed, about 10 minutes. Or prepare a medium-hot grill and cook them on the grill. Transfer them to a bowl and cover with aluminum foil. Let sit for 10 minutes.

In a roasting pan or ovenproof skillet, toss the broccoli with 2 tablespoons of the olive oil and ½ teaspoon of the salt. Roast the broccoli until it's browned but still slightly crunchy, about 10 minutes, stirring once halfway through.

Cut the eggplant in half lengthwise and scoop the flesh into a large bowl. Whisk in the remaining 2 tablespoons olive oil, the lemon zest and juice, the remaining ¼ teaspoon salt, and the red pepper flakes. If you don't like the eggplant seeds, push the mixture through a fine-mesh strainer. Toss in the broccoli and marjoram leaves, coating them with the puree. Sprinkle the cheese over the top and serve warm or at room temperature.

MUSHROOM, WALNUT, AND FENNEL SALAD

with Parmigiano

THANKS TO A MOUNTAIN of mushrooms and a shower of Parmigiano, this fall lunch or light dinner salad is full of deep, umami-rich, satisfying flavor. Beech mushrooms have a woodsy flavor and cook up fast, but feel free to use readily available creminis instead. You can prepare the mushrooms and mushroom-walnut puree up to a day ahead, then toss everything together just before serving.

SERVES 4 · ACTIVE: 25 MIN · TOTAL: 25 MIN

1 pound brown beech or cremini mushrooms

¾ cup extra-virgin olive oil, plus more for serving

1 shallot, diced

1 garlic clove, chopped

Fine sea salt and freshly ground black pepper

1 cup walnut halves, toasted

2 tablespoons black vinegar or malt vinegar

1 tablespoon balsamic vinegar

1 fennel bulb

Finely grated zest and juice of 1 lemon

4 ounces Parmigiano-Reggiano, grated

Remove the base of the mushroom stems. Cut beech mushrooms into large bite-size pieces, or quarter the creminis.

Heat 2 tablespoons of the olive oil in a large skillet over medium heat. Add the mushrooms and shallot and cook for 2 minutes, tossing every 30 seconds. Add the garlic and cook for another minute. Season with salt and pepper to taste, and remove the pan from the heat.

In a blender, combine ½ cup of the cooked mushrooms and shallot, 2 tablespoons of the toasted walnut halves, the black vinegar, and balsamic vinegar. With the blender on, pour in ½ cup of the olive oil in a slow, steady stream until the mixture is smooth and spreadable. Season with salt and pepper to taste.

Cut the stalks off the fennel bulb, reserving ¼ cup of the fronds for the salad. Remove and discard the outer layer of the bulb. Thinly slice the fennel crosswise with a mandoline or sharp knife.

In a large bowl, toss together the sliced fennel, the remaining mushrooms, the remaining toasted walnuts, the lemon zest and juice, the remaining 2 tablespoons olive oil, the reserved fennel fronds, half of the cheese, and salt and pepper to taste.

To serve, spread a large dollop of mushroom-walnut puree in the center of each plate and top with a portion of the salad, a sprinkling of the remaining cheese, and a drizzle of olive oil.

MUSHROOM AND ARUGULA BUCKWHEAT CREPES

A SAVORY CREPE STUFFED with mushrooms and greens with Parmigiano is a hearty vegetarian lunch and a change of pace from sandwiches or salads. I love the woodsy flavor of chanterelles, but they're pricey, so I mix them with other mushrooms—any combination works—and enrich the dish with a generous drizzle of warm goat cheese fondue.

SERVES 4 TO 6 · ACTIVE: 15 MIN · TOTAL: 20 MIN

Butter, for greasing the pan

2 tablespoons extra-virgin olive oil

1 shallot, finely chopped (about ¼ cup)

1 pound mushrooms (shiitakes, baby bellas, chanterelles), cut into ¼-inch slices

1 teaspoon finely chopped garlic

Fine sea salt and freshly ground black pepper

2 tablespoons dry white wine

4 cups loosely packed baby arugula

¼ cup plus 2 tablespoons freshly grated Parmigiano-Reggiano

1 tablespoon chopped fresh rosemary

1 tablespoon sliced fresh flat-leaf parsley

4 to 6 Buckwheat Crepes (page 94)

½ cup Warm Goat Cheese Fondue (page 288; optional)

Preheat the oven to 325°F. Lightly butter a casserole dish.

In a large sauté pan, heat the olive oil over medium heat. When the oil is hot, add the shallots. They should sizzle a little. Add the mushrooms, garlic, two to three large pinches of salt, and four turns of black pepper. Cook the mushrooms until tender and any water they release has evaporated, 5 to 10 minutes, tossing about once every minute.

Add the wine and cook until it evaporates, about 2 minutes. Toss in the arugula and cook until wilted, about 2 minutes. Remove the pan from the heat and stir in ¼ cup of the cheese and the rosemary and parsley. Taste and adjust the seasoning, and let the filling cool briefly.

To assemble, divide the filling evenly among the crepes, piling it in a horizontal line a couple of inches from the bottom edge of each crepe. Being careful not to tear them, roll the crepes tightly from the bottom to the top, like a cigar. Arrange the filled crepes in one layer in the casserole dish. Sprinkle the remaining 2 tablespoons cheese over the top and bake until the cheese has melted, about 5 minutes. Drizzle the goat cheese fondue over the crepes for extra richness, and serve immediately.

BUCKWHEAT CREPES

THANKS TO THE EARTHY, grainy nature of buckwheat, these aren't as delicate as regular crepes and can stand up to fillings with bolder flavors and sturdy greens, like sautéed arugula or kale. Chopped rosemary or thyme can replace the chives. If you want a sweet crepe, omit the herb and add 2 teaspoons sugar to the batter.

MAKES 4 TO 6 LARGE CREPES · ACTIVE: 15 MIN · TOTAL: 25 MIN

1 cup buckwheat flour

Fine sea salt

1 tablespoon finely sliced fresh chives

3 large eggs

1 cup whole milk

4 tablespoons unsalted butter;
1 tablespoon melted

In a blender, combine the flour, a large pinch of salt, the chives, eggs, milk, and melted butter. Mix on low speed until the batter comes together.

To make the crepes, melt ½ tablespoon of the remaining butter in a large (9-inch minimum) seasoned or nonstick sauté pan over medium heat until the butter begins to foam. Pour 3 ounces of batter into the center of the pan and quickly tilt it in a circular motion to spread the batter into a large, thin circle—the thinner, the better. Cook until the batter firms up, about 2 minutes. Using a rubber spatula, carefully loosen the edges of the crepe and flip it. Cook for 1 minute more. Flip the crepe out onto a piece of parchment paper or a large plate.

Wipe out the pan and repeat with the remaining butter and batter, layering each cooked crepe between pieces of parchment paper. If not using the crepes right away, cover the stack with plastic wrap and refrigerate for up to 24 hours.

MUSHROOMS AND FENNEL

en Papillote

WE ALL KNOW HOW good sautéed and roasted mushrooms are, but don't forget about steaming them—this method showcases their flavor. It doesn't get much easier than this dish, and you can switch it up with a variety of mushrooms; add herbs like cilantro, parsley, or thyme; or toss in a little grated lemon zest. For a nice touch at a dinner party, divide the mushroom mixture among four individual parchment pouches and let guests cut open their own pouch at the table.

SERVES 4 · ACTIVE: 15 MIN · TOTAL: 30 MIN

6 cups mixed mushrooms, cleaned, trimmed, and cut into 1- to 2-inch pieces

3 scallions or ramps, sliced

½ fennel bulb, thinly sliced

3 tablespoons tamari or soy sauce

2 tablespoons Roasted Garlic Puree (page 77), or 1 tablespoon minced garlic

1 tablespoon extra-virgin olive oil

½ teaspoon ground fennel

Preheat the oven to 350°F.

Toss all of the ingredients together in a large bowl. Cut parchment paper into a 12-inch circle and place it in an 8-inch pie plate or a shallow glass casserole dish.

Pour the mushroom mixture into the center of the paper. Make a pouch by bringing the edges of the paper together and tying with a piece of kitchen twine.

Bake until the pouch puffs out, about 15 minutes. Transfer the packet to a serving platter and cut open the top of the pouch. Serve immediately.

SUMMER SQUASH

with Feta, Cured Olives, Chickpeas, and Nasturtiums

THIS IS A GREAT summer dish with the familiar flavors of a Greek salad. It's light because the squash is raw, but the crispy chickpeas add substance and richness. Choose small zucchini and squash that feel heavy for their size—they'll add more high-impact crunch and fresh flavor. Watercress has a peppery bite similar to nasturtium leaves, so it makes a good substitute.

SERVES 4 TO 6 · ACTIVE: 10 MIN · TOTAL: 20 MIN

2 zucchini (no longer than 6 inches)

2 yellow summer squash (no longer than 6 inches)

1 tablespoon extra-virgin olive oil

Finely grated zest and juice of 1 lemon

¼ teaspoon fine sea salt

Freshly ground black pepper

1½ cups Crispy Chickpeas with Rosemary (page 82)

4 ounces feta cheese, preferably sheep's milk feta, crumbled

¼ cup black olives, pitted and chopped

¼ cup fresh basil leaves, sliced

4 nasturtium leaves, sliced, or watercress sprigs

Remove the stems and ends of the zucchini and yellow squash and slice into ¼-inch-thick rounds.

In a large bowl, toss the squash with the olive oil, lemon zest and juice, salt, and four turns of black pepper. Let marinate for 10 minutes.

Add the chickpeas, feta, olives, basil, and nasturtium leaves and toss. Serve immediately.

GOAT CHEESE GNOCCHI

with Basil, Lemon, and Baby Summer Squash

DON'T LET THE LENGTH of this recipe deter you—this is a relatively simple approach to gnocchi using basic, readily available ingredients. Made with pâte à choux—the same dough that adds airiness to profiteroles and cream puffs—these pillowy Parisienne gnocchi are lighter than Italian potato-based gnocchi, so they pair well with spring vegetables.

SERVES 4 · ACTIVE: 2 HR · TOTAL: 2 HR 30 MIN

Fine sea salt

1½ sticks (12 tablespoons) unsalted butter

2 cups all-purpose flour

12 ounces goat cheese

5 large eggs

3 tablespoons finely sliced fresh basil plus 1 cup fresh basil leaves, coarsely chopped, plus whole leaves for garnish (mixed varieties of basil work great)

Freshly ground black pepper

1 pound baby summer squash, cut into bite-size pieces

1 tablespoon vegetable oil, plus more if needed

1 tablespoon extra-virgin olive oil

1 garlic clove, minced, or 1 tablespoon Roasted Garlic Puree (page 77)

¼ cup Vegetable Stock (page 292)

Finely grated zest and juice of 1 lemon

5 scallions, chopped

½ cup freshly grated Parmigiano-Reggiano

Bring 6 quarts water and 1 teaspoon salt to a simmer in a large pot.

In a medium pot, bring 1½ cups water, the butter, and 1 teaspoon salt to a boil. Add the flour, reduce the heat to low, and stir with a wooden spoon for about 2 minutes, until the mixture becomes a smooth dough and doesn't stick to the bottom of the pot.

Remove the pot of dough from the heat and stir in 8 ounces of the goat cheese. Crack the eggs in one at a time, beating each one into the dough before adding the next. The batter should be sticky. Stir in the finely sliced basil and two turns of black pepper.

Transfer one-quarter of the batter to a pastry bag with a #5 tip (⁷⁄₁₆-inch), or a gallon-size zipper-lock bag with ½ inch cut off of one corner.

[RECIPE CONTINUES]

Hold the bag over the pot of simmering water and squeeze the batter out in ½-inch cylinder dumplings, cutting them with a paring knife so they fall into the water. Simmer for 4 minutes. Once all gnocchi have floated to the top, cook for 2 more minutes. Remove the gnocchi from the water with a slotted spoon and transfer to a paper towel–lined baking sheet to remove any excess water.

Repeat with the remaining dough in three more batches. (Once cooled, the gnocchi can be used immediately, or refrigerated for up to 2 days.)

Bring a large pot of salted water to a boil. Add the squash and cook until tender, about 5 minutes. Drain.

In a large nonstick sauté pan, heat the vegetable oil over high heat. Working in batches, add as many gnocchi to the pan as will fit in one layer without overcrowding. Brown the gnocchi for 3 to 4 minutes on each side. Transfer to a plate. Brown the remaining gnocchi, adding another tablespoon of vegetable oil to the pan in between batches, if needed.

Carefully wipe out any remaining vegetable oil from the pan with a paper towel. Heat the olive oil over medium heat. Add the garlic and cook for 1 minute without browning. Add the vegetable stock and lemon zest and juice, and bring to a simmer. Add the squash, gnocchi, scallions, cheese, and coarsely chopped basil leaves and toss. Cook just long enough for everything to get hot.

Transfer to a warm serving dish and sprinkle the remaining goat cheese on top. Garnish with whole basil leaves and a couple of turns of black pepper. Serve immediately.

RATATOUILLE

with Baked Duck Eggs

THERE ARE TWO WAYS to approach ratatouille: Cook all the vegetables together like a stew, or cook them each separately. I'm in the latter camp. Giving the vegetables individual attention may take longer, but I'm after the sear and caramelization that develop by cooking them separately. It brings out the individual flavors of each vegetable and gives the final dish layers of flavor. Every time I make this, I wish I'd doubled it—it only gets better after a day or two in the fridge (minus the duck egg, of course!).

SERVES 4 · ACTIVE: 40 MIN · TOTAL: 1 HR

½ cup extra-virgin olive oil

1 large white onion, halved through the core and thinly sliced

1 red bell pepper, seeds and stem removed, cut into ¼-inch slices

4 plum tomatoes, seeded and coarsely chopped

¼ cup dry white wine

1 tablespoon Roasted Garlic Puree (page 77), or 3 garlic cloves, finely chopped

Fine sea salt

Red pepper flakes

1 small zucchini, cut into large dice

1 small yellow summer squash, cut into large dice

Freshly ground black pepper

1 small Japanese eggplant, cut into large dice

1 tablespoon chopped fresh marjoram or oregano

1 tablespoon chopped fresh lemon thyme or thyme

1 tablespoon sliced fresh flat-leaf parsley

1 teaspoon finely grated lemon zest

6 tablespoons freshly grated Parmigiano-Reggiano

4 duck or large chicken eggs

In a medium saucepan, heat ¼ cup of the olive oil over medium-low heat. Add the onion and bell pepper and stew until tender, about 5 minutes. Add the tomatoes, wine, garlic, a pinch of salt, and a small pinch of red pepper flakes. Reduce the heat to low and continue cooking, stirring occasionally.

While the tomatoes and peppers stew, heat 1 tablespoon of the olive oil in a large sauté pan over medium heat. Sauté the zucchini and yellow squash with a pinch of salt and two turns of black pepper until they're lightly brown and tender, about 4 minutes. Stir the zucchini and squash into the tomato mixture.

{ RECIPE CONTINUES }

In the same sauté pan, heat 2 tablespoons of the olive oil over medium heat and cook the eggplant with a pinch of salt and two turns of black pepper until lightly browned, about 5 minutes. Add the eggplant to the tomato mixture.

Stew all the vegetables together over low heat until the tomatoes are broken down and the vegetables are tender but not mushy, about 30 minutes. Add the marjoram, thyme, and parsley and continue cooking for another 5 minutes. Take the pan off the heat and stir in the lemon zest and 2 tablespoons of the cheese. Taste and adjust the seasoning with salt and pepper to taste.

Preheat the oven to 325°F.

Distribute the vegetables evenly into 4 (8-ounce) ovenproof ramekins. Make a ½-inch well in the center of each ramekin and crack an egg into the well. Sprinkle 1 tablespoon of Parmigiano over each egg. Place the ramekins on a baking sheet and bake until the cheese has melted, about 7 minutes. Serve immediately.

JERKED BUTTERNUT SQUASH

I LIVE NOT FAR from several Caribbean neighborhoods in Brooklyn, where the spicy scent of jerk seasoning coming from sidewalk grills in the summer makes my mouth water. My take on jerk isn't as fiery, but it's every bit as boldly flavored and delicious.

SERVES 8 · ACTIVE: 20 MIN · TOTAL: 40 MIN

2 tablespoons light brown sugar

2 tablespoons paprika

1 tablespoon dried chives

1 teaspoon ground thyme

½ teaspoon ground cinnamon

½ teaspoon ground allspice

½ teaspoon onion powder

½ teaspoon garlic powder

⅛ teaspoon ground nutmeg

⅛ teaspoon cayenne pepper

Fine sea salt and freshly ground
    black pepper

¼ cup extra-virgin olive oil

¼ cup sour cream

Zest and juice of 1 lime

½ cup fresh cilantro leaves, sliced

2 tablespoons extra-virgin olive oil

1 large butternut squash

Preheat the oven to 425°F. Line two 9 x 11-inch baking pans or one 13 x 18-inch pan with aluminum foil and place them on the bottom rack of the oven. Heat the pans for at least 10 minutes.

In a large bowl, combine the brown sugar, paprika, chives, thyme, cinnamon, allspice, onion powder, garlic powder, nutmeg, and cayenne. Add 2 teaspoons salt, 1 teaspoon black pepper, and the olive oil. Stir together until combined.

In a small bowl, stir together the sour cream, lime zest and juice, cilantro, olive oil, ⅛ teaspoon salt, and two turns of black pepper. Refrigerate until needed.

Cut the butternut squash in half crosswise where the bulb meets the straight top. Peel the skin off the top and bulb with a sharp vegetable peeler. Cut each piece in half lengthwise and scrape the seeds out of the bulb with a spoon. Cut the pieces in half lengthwise and slice into 1-inch-thick pieces the shape of a quarter circle. Toss the squash in the bowl with the spices, coating the pieces well on all sides.

Arrange the squash flat side down in the preheated baking pans in one even layer. Roast until the bottom of the squash has a dark brown, almost blackened crust and the pieces are tender when poked in the center with a fork, about 20 minutes. Serve the squash blackened side up with the sauce drizzled over the top.

DELICATA SQUASH

with Honey and Red Pepper Flakes

MOST WINTER SQUASH VARIETIES are large and dense with tough skins, but delicata squashes are fairly small and have a thin skin that doesn't need to be peeled. Tossed in honey and a sprinkling of red pepper flakes, pan-roasted slices of delicata quickly become tender and sweet, with a little zing of heat.

SERVES 6 · ACTIVE: 15 MIN · TOTAL: 15 MIN

2 pounds delicata squash

2 tablespoons extra-virgin olive oil, plus more if needed

⅛ teaspoon fine sea salt

2 tablespoons orange blossom honey

1 teaspoon freshly squeezed lemon juice

1 tablespoon finely sliced fresh chives

⅛ teaspoon red pepper flakes

Freshly ground black pepper

Remove the ends of the squash and quarter the squash lengthwise into 4 long spears. Scrape out and discard the seeds and loose flesh with a spoon. Cut the squash into ¼-inch-thick pieces the shape of a quarter circle.

In a large sauté pan, heat the olive oil over high heat until it starts to quiver. To test the temperature, add one piece of squash to the pan—it should immediately sizzle. Add the rest of the squash and toss with the salt. (If necessary, cook in batches to avoid overcrowding the pan.)

Toss the squash about once a minute, sautéing until it becomes golden brown and tender, 5 to 8 minutes. If the pan seems dry, add another tablespoon of oil. Add the honey, lemon juice, chives, red pepper flakes, and four turns of black pepper. Toss to combine, and continue cooking for another 2 minutes. Taste and adjust the seasoning, if necessary. Serve immediately.

SPAGHETTI SQUASH

with Sage and Maple Syrup

SPAGHETTI SQUASH IS VERY mild and has an interesting texture. Its draw is all about the silky spaghetti-like strands of flesh tossed with a few flavorful companions—in this case, a light balance of maple syrup, tart sherry vinegar, and woodsy sage. This version pairs well with roasted salmon, poultry, or pork.

SERVES 4 · ACTIVE: 20 MIN · TOTAL: I HR 40 MIN

1 cup Vegetable Stock (page 292) or water, plus more if needed

¼ cup maple syrup

4 tablespoons unsalted butter, cut into pieces

2 whole cloves

1 fresh bay leaf

1 large spaghetti squash, halved lengthwise and seeded

Fine sea salt and freshly ground black pepper

2 tablespoons sherry vinegar

1 tablespoon extra-virgin olive oil

1 tablespoon finely chopped shallots

2 tablespoons chopped fresh sage

Preheat the oven to 325°F.

In a casserole dish large enough to fit the squash halves, whisk together the vegetable stock and maple syrup. Add the butter, cloves, and bay leaf.

Season the squash flesh with ¼ teaspoon salt and a few turns of black pepper. Place the squash cut side down in the casserole dish and cover with aluminum foil. Bake for 1 hour. Remove the foil; there still should be a little liquid in the dish. If not, add ¼ cup more vegetable stock. Bake uncovered until the squash feels like a perfectly ripe peach when poked, or a paring knife has no resistance when inserted, another 10 to 20 minutes.

Remove the squash from the liquid and let it rest cut side down until it's cool enough to handle.

Meanwhile, strain the cooking liquid from the casserole dish through a fine-mesh sieve into a medium bowl. There should be about ¼ cup of liquid. Add vinegar, olive oil, shallots, sage, a pinch of salt, and one turn of black pepper, and whisk to combine.

To remove the squash flesh, turn the squash so it's cut side up and scrape with a fork from top to bottom. Transfer the long, stringy strands to the bowl with the vinaigrette and toss. Season with salt and pepper to taste and serve warm, at room temperature, or chilled.

BABY BLUE HUBBARD SQUASH SOUP

with Blue Cheese and Pickled Pears

WHEN YOUR LOCAL FARMERS' market is brimming with winter squash, don't neglect some of the funkier-looking varieties, like Hubbard squash. It's a beautiful blue winter squash that grows to be fairly enormous and unwieldy, so you definitely want a baby one. The sweet, creamy orange flesh in a Hubbard is perfect for roasting. Here it is cooked on the stovetop with the other ingredients and pureed. Add salty blue cheese and crisp pears and it's a stunning soup. This freezes well, so you can easily use the whole squash and double the recipe for a big batch.

SERVES 4 TO 6 · ACTIVE: 20 MIN · TOTAL: 1 HR

4 tablespoons unsalted butter

2 celery stalks, diced

1 large shallot, diced

1 small garlic clove, chopped

½ baby blue Hubbard squash (or, if Hubbard is not available, 1 large butternut squash), peeled and diced (about 3 cups)

2 tablespoons dry white wine

2 quarts Vegetable Stock (page 292) or Chicken Stock (page 293), plus more if needed

1 thyme sprig

1 bay leaf

1 red Bartlett pear

2 tablespoons white wine vinegar

1 teaspoon honey

1 tablespoon extra-virgin olive oil

Fine sea salt and freshly ground white pepper

4 ounces blue cheese, crumbled

In a large pot over medium-low heat, melt the butter and cook the celery, shallot, and garlic until the shallot is translucent. Add the squash and wine and cook until the wine has mostly evaporated, about 2 minutes. Add the stock, thyme, and bay leaf. Raise the heat to medium, bring to a low simmer, and cook until the vegetables are tender, 35 to 40 minutes.

Core the pear and slice it into matchstick-size pieces, about 2 inches long. In a bowl, toss the pear with the vinegar, honey, olive oil, and a pinch of salt. Set aside.

Puree the soup in a blender until smooth and creamy (you may need to do this in batches). Adjust the consistency with more stock, if needed. Season to taste with salt and white pepper.

Ladle the soup into warm soup bowls or a tureen and garnish with blue cheese and the pickled pears.

The Blank Plate

Stay close to nature. It will never fail you.
FRANK LLOYD WRIGHT

I had to learn a lot about food only to try to forget it, and the way I plate food is a prime example. Haute cuisine, the style of high-end cooking I was trained in, meant transforming ingredients into complicated presentations far removed from their original forms. But those meticulous, time-consuming techniques added nothing to the flavor of the dish, so I left them behind. The cook's job is to showcase ingredients without obscuring them. Here are a few simple ways to make your dishes look their best.

FOLLOW NATURE: Accentuate the natural form of your ingredients. Cut vegetables into shapes that retain their natural look, and leave skins and stems on when they're palatable. We eat with our eyes first, and food that bears a relationship to its natural form will seem more immediately flavorful and delicious.

USE WHITE SPACE: The white (unused) space on the plate helps focus attention on the natural vibrancy and textures of the food. Use an oversize plate or platter that will allow some white space. Most home plates are smaller than the plates used in restaurants.

FRAME IT: By simply "framing" the food with greens or herbs, you will be able to make a simple dish like a grilled piece of meat or fish stand out. Look for ingredients that are already in the recipe, like an herb, vegetable, or green. Use watercress for fish or chicken and herbs like fresh rosemary or thyme for roasted items—ingredients that add color and complement the dish. Be resourceful and use parts of the plant that you might normally discard, like the tough outer leaves of cabbages and greens or fennel fronds, carrot tops, or beet greens.

SLICE MEAT CAREFULLY: Leave individual portions of roasted meats like a pork chop or steak unsliced for a more dramatic presentation. But for pork tenderloin, hanger steak, lamb sirloin, and other cuts that don't look so attractive whole, slicing is the way to go. Slicing also contrasts the dark outer color with the pink, juicy interior. Thin slices cut against the grain also make the meat more tender. Transfer the meat to a cutting board and slice with a long, sharp knife, letting the slices naturally fall in a line. Use a large spatula to transfer the slices to the serving dish.

DON'T FORGET TO FINISH: Add an attractive and flavorful ingredient to the dish as a final garnish, like a fresh herb sprig or a drizzle of oil. For more ideas, see Finishing (page 140). ❖

QUICK-PICKLED CUMIN CARROTS

THIS IS ONE OF the most versatile staple condiments in my kitchen. It adds a crunchy zip of brightness to heavy, rich dishes like barbecued and braised meats and livens up sandwiches, burgers, and creamy soups.

MAKES ABOUT 2 CUPS · ACTIVE: 20 MIN · TOTAL: 50 MIN

8 ounces carrots, preferably heirloom

1 teaspoon cumin seeds, slightly crushed

½ cup rice vinegar

2 tablespoons mirin or light honey

1 garlic clove, smashed

1 teaspoon whole black peppercorns

2 teaspoons fine sea salt

Shred the carrots lengthwise into ribbons using a sharp vegetable peeler. Place the ribbons in a heatproof glass bowl.

Heat a 2-quart pot over medium heat. When the pot is warm, add the cumin seeds and toss frequently until they start to barely smoke, about 3 minutes. Carefully add the vinegar (it might splatter a bit), along with 1 cup water, the mirin, garlic, peppercorns, and salt, and bring to a boil. Pour the hot pickling liquid into the bowl of carrot ribbons. Cool uncovered at room temperature for 30 minutes to 1 hour (the longer, the better).

Store the carrots completely covered in the pickling liquid in an airtight container in the refrigerator for up to 1 month, or at room temperature.

ROASTED CARROTS, PARSNIPS, AND BELGIAN ENDIVE

with Curry and Currants

IT'S HIGHLY POSSIBLE THAT this tumble of sweet oven-roasted carrots and parsnips, bitter endive, and earthy curry will steal the spotlight from the main course on your table. For extra crunch, toss in sunflower seeds or chopped walnuts.

If possible, buy carrots with the greens attached, even if they'll be trimmed off. They're likely to be fresher than loose carrots. Also, there's a lot of flavor in the peel, so I leave it on when using small or medium carrots.

SERVES 4 TO 6 · ACTIVE: 15 MIN · TOTAL: 1 HR

½ cup carrot juice or water

2 tablespoons extra-virgin olive oil

1½ tablespoons curry powder

½ teaspoon fine sea salt

Freshly ground black pepper

1 bunch medium carrots (about 1 pound), trimmed and cut into ½-inch pieces

1 pound parsnips, peeled and cut into ½-inch pieces

¼ cup dried black currants

2 heads Belgian endive, ends trimmed, cut crosswise into ½-inch pieces

1 tablespoon sliced fresh flat-leaf parsley

Preheat the oven to 350°F.

In a large bowl, whisk together the carrot juice, olive oil, curry powder, salt, and four turns of black pepper. Toss the carrots and parsnips in the bowl to coat them with the liquid. Transfer them to a large baking dish and cover with aluminum foil. Roast for 30 minutes.

Remove the foil and stir in the currants and endive. Roast uncovered until the carrots and parsnips are golden brown and the endive is wilted, about 15 minutes more. Season with salt and pepper to taste. Sprinkle with the parsley and serve.

SHERRY-GLAZED CARROTS AND RADISHES

SWEET CARROTS PAIR WELL with another root crop: peppery radishes. Radishes are especially quick and easy to grow (about 3 weeks from seed to radish), so I usually have an abundance of them in my garden in the spring. They're often overlooked as a vegetable for cooking, but I like how heat mellows their sharp flavor and softens them. Using radishes and carrots of different shapes, colors, and sizes here makes for a memorable side dish. Served with a nice piece of grilled fish, it's a perfect meal in 30 minutes.

SERVES 4 · ACTIVE: 30 MIN · TOTAL: 30 MIN

2 tablespoons extra-virgin olive oil

8 ounces carrots, mixed colors, tops trimmed, peeled, and cut into bite-size pieces

8 ounces mixed radishes (French Breakfast, watermelon, or red radishes), trimmed and quartered lengthwise

¼ cup sherry vinegar

2 tablespoons freshly squeezed orange juice

2 tablespoons honey

Fine sea salt and freshly ground black pepper

1 tablespoon chopped fresh chives

Heat the olive oil in a large skillet over medium heat. Add the carrots and pan-roast them, stirring occasionally, until they start to brown, about 10 minutes. Add the radishes and cook for 3 minutes, tossing frequently. Add the vinegar, orange juice, and honey and cook until the radishes and carrots are al dente and fully coated with the glaze, about 5 minutes.

Season with salt and pepper to taste. Stir in the chives and serve hot or at room temperature.

NAPA CABBAGE SLAW

with Sriracha Aioli

NAPA CABBAGE IS LIGHTER and less cumbersome to eat than regular cabbage, and I love how its spongy, crinkly leaves grab onto vinaigrettes and sauces, like the spicy aioli here. Serve a heaping bowl of this slaw with grilled meats or fish.

SERVES 4 TO 6 · ACTIVE: 20 MIN · TOTAL: 20 MIN

For the aioli:

2 large eggs, at room temperature

1 tablespoon sriracha

1 tablespoon freshly squeezed lemon
　juice

1 teaspoon soy sauce or tamari

Freshly ground black pepper

1 cup vegetable oil

For the slaw:

1 head napa cabbage, thinly sliced

¼ cup cilantro sprigs, coarsely chopped

¼ cup thinly sliced scallions

To make the aioli: Place the eggs, sriracha, lemon juice, soy sauce, and two turns of black pepper in a blender and blend for 1 minute. With the blender running, slowly pour in half of the oil. Stop to scrape down the sides. With the blender running again, pour in the rest of the oil in a slow, steady stream. Taste and adjust the seasoning as needed. Reserve 1 cup for the slaw and refrigerate the remaining aioli for use in other recipes for up to 3 days.

To make the slaw: In a large bowl, toss the cabbage with the aioli until fully coated. Add the cilantro and scallions and toss. Taste and adjust the seasoning as needed, and serve.

BABY BOK CHOY

with Roasted Red Pepper Sauce

THESE DAYS, OVEN-ROASTED VEGETABLES are common fare—they pack in lots of caramelized flavor without a lot of effort. Expand your repertoire and try oven-roasting leafy cabbages, too. The outer leaves become crispy and maybe even a little charred, the cores are tender with a bit of crunch, and the whole head takes on a mildly sweet flavor that pairs well with just about anything. If using regular, mature bok choy, cut it lengthwise into quarters and roast for an additional 5 to 10 minutes.

SERVES 4 TO 6 · ACTIVE: 5 MIN · TOTAL: 20 MIN

1 tablespoon plus 1 teaspoon extra-virgin olive oil

4 heads baby bok choy (about 6 inches long), halved lengthwise

Fine sea salt and freshly ground white pepper

Roasted Red Pepper Sauce (page 289)

¼ cup sliced scallions

¼ cup cilantro sprigs

Preheat the oven to 375°F.

Heat the oil in a roasting pan for about 5 minutes. Lightly season the bok choy all over with salt and white pepper.

Arrange the bok choy cut side down in the pan and roast until golden brown and tender, about 5 minutes on each side. Drizzle the red pepper sauce over the bok choy. Sprinkle with the scallions and cilantro sprigs and serve.

ROASTED BRUSSELS SPROUTS

with Apples, Pistachios, and Bacon

BRUSSELS SPROUTS HAVE BECOME a mainstay on every farm-to-table menu in Brooklyn. You can find them served in towering piles, roasted or fried, and dressed with everything from sriracha and fish sauce to mustard and Parmigiano-Reggiano. I love their nutty flavor when roasted, and tossing in tart apples and crunchy bacon makes for a sweet, salty, smoky combination. This dish reminds you that vegetables can and should be indulgent at times. Turn this into a hash by slicing the sprouts in a food processor, or drape a poached egg on top and call it brunch.

SERVES 4 TO 6 · ACTIVE: 20 MIN · TOTAL: 1 HR

1 tablespoon vegetable oil, preferably avocado oil

4 slices bacon, preferably a heritage breed, cut into ½-inch pieces

1 pound Brussels sprouts, outer leaves removed and quartered

1 large shallot, thinly sliced

¼ teaspoon fine sea salt

2 red apples, cored and diced into ½-inch cubes (about 2 cups)

¼ cup shelled crushed pistachios

Finely grated zest and juice of ½ lemon

1 tablespoon finely sliced fresh chives

Freshly ground black pepper

Preheat the oven to 350°F.

Place the vegetable oil in a 9 x 11-inch baking dish and put in the oven for 5 minutes to heat.

Add the bacon to the dish, return to the oven, and cook until it starts to brown, about 5 minutes. Add the Brussels sprouts, shallot, and salt to the dish and toss to coat the vegetables in the bacon fat and oil. Bake until the sprouts are light golden brown, about 30 minutes, stirring every 10 minutes. Toss in the apples and pistachios and bake for another 10 minutes. Stir in the lemon zest and juice, chives, and four turns of black pepper. Taste and adjust the seasoning as needed, and serve.

BEET RISOTTO

with Goat Cheese and Dill

THE STUNNING PINK COLOR of this risotto comes from fresh beet juice, which is an easy find around Brooklyn thanks to all the fresh juice shops that have cropped up in the past few years. Using beet juice along with chopped, roasted beets allows their slight sweetness to weave throughout the entire dish. I'm partial to Vialone Nano rice, rather than the traditional Arborio; I find it makes the creamiest risotto. If you don't have access to fresh beet juice in your area, peel and grate one red beet, and add it to the rice after you pour in the wine.

SERVES 4 · ACTIVE: 40 MIN · TOTAL: 40 MIN

2 tablespoons extra-virgin olive oil

1 cup Vialone Nano or Arborio rice

Fine sea salt and freshly ground
　　black pepper

4 tablespoons unsalted butter, cubed

1 garlic clove, finely chopped

1 shallot, finely chopped

½ cup white wine

2½ cups Vegetable Stock (page 292),
　　heated, or hot water

½ cup fresh beet juice

1 cup roasted beets, cut into
　　bite-size pieces

½ cup goat cheese

½ cup finely grated Parmigiano-
　　Reggiano

1 tablespoon chopped fresh dill

1 tablespoon sliced fresh chives

¼ cup Warm Goat Cheese Fondue
　　(page 288; optional)

In a large saucepan, heat the olive oil over medium heat until hot but not smoking. Add the rice and toast, stirring frequently, until it turns from opaque white to pearly white, about 5 minutes. Be sure not to let it brown. Add a pinch of salt and a few turns of black pepper.

Reduce the heat to medium-low and melt 2 tablespoons of the butter in the saucepan, then add the garlic and shallot. Cook until the shallots are translucent but not brown, about 3 minutes. Add the wine and continue stirring until the liquid is almost completely evaporated.

Pour in half the stock and cook, stirring frequently, until it's absorbed by the rice, about 5 minutes. Add the rest of the stock and continue cooking and stirring to release the starch. Cook until the rice is al dente and all of the stock is completely absorbed, about 5 minutes.

Stir in the beet juice and beets and cook for another few minutes, stirring constantly now, until the beet juice is absorbed. Stir in the goat cheese, the remaining 2 tablespoons butter, and the Parmigiano, and sprinkle with the dill and chives. Drizzle with the goat cheese fondue, if using. Taste and adjust the seasoning as needed. Serve immediately.

GOLDEN BEET BROTH

with Goat Cheese and Beet Dumplings

I'VE TAKEN A COUPLE of liberties with the classic Russian borscht by using golden beets instead of red and vegetable stock instead of beef stock. This soup has a beautiful, light golden broth with a consommé feel to it. Lush goat cheese dumplings keep the soup from being too spare and offer a new way to experience the typical beet–goat cheese pairing. If you can't get beets with the greens attached, you can substitute any type of cooking greens you have.

SERVES 4 · ACTIVE: 20 MIN · TOTAL: 40 MIN

1 bunch golden baby beets with greens

1 tablespoon extra-virgin olive oil

1 large shallot, thinly sliced

2 teaspoons honey

4 cups Vegetable Stock (page 292)

2 teaspoons fine sea salt

2 thyme sprigs

1 fresh bay leaf

1 garlic clove, lightly crushed

2 whole cloves

2 tablespoons rice vinegar

12 Goat Cheese and Beet Dumplings (page 126)

Chive Oil (page 25), for garnish

Peel the beets. Cut the beet greens into ribbons—you only need 1 cup of ribbons, so compost or discard the rest (or sauté to eat on their own). Reserve a few of the stems from the greens for the dumpling mixture. Quarter the beets into bite-size wedges.

In a medium saucepan, heat the olive oil over low heat and cook the shallot and quartered beets for 5 minutes, stirring occasionally. Add the honey and cook until it starts to bubble, about 2 minutes. Add the vegetable stock and bring to a gentle simmer. Add the salt.

Put the thyme, bay leaf, garlic, and cloves in a tea ball or cheesecloth pouch tied with kitchen string and place in the broth. Simmer until the beets are fork-tender, about 20 minutes. Add the beet greens and cook for another 5 minutes. Stir in the vinegar and taste and adjust the seasoning as needed.

Place 3 goat cheese dumplings in each warm serving bowl and ladle the hot soup over them. Let sit for 2 to 3 minutes. Finish the soup by drizzling a little chive oil into each bowl for flavor and color.

GOAT CHEESE AND BEET DUMPLINGS

MAKES ABOUT 12 DUMPLINGS · ACTIVE: 25 MIN · TOTAL: 25 MIN

1 cup goat cheese

1 large egg

2 tablespoons minced beet stems (reserved from the bunch used to make the broth) or fresh flat-leaf parsley

1 tablespoon sliced fresh chives or scallions

1 teaspoon finely grated lemon zest

½ teaspoon fine sea salt

Freshly ground black pepper

¼ cup all-purpose flour

In a medium bowl, mix the goat cheese with the egg until combined. Stir in the beet stems, chives, lemon zest, salt, and six turns of black pepper. Sift in the flour and stir until just combined.

Bring a large pot of salted water to a very light simmer. Dip 2 teaspoons into the water and then make a dumpling by scooping out a teaspoon of the cheese mixture and shaping it with the spoons. Working in batches of 6 at a time, drop the dumplings into the water and cook for 2 to 4 minutes, until the dumplings float. Remove with a slotted spoon, shake off any water, and place in the serving bowl being used. If not using right away, cool the dumplings in ice water before refrigerating in an airtight container for up to 1 day, and when serving reheat in the soup until warm.

BABY BEET SALAD

with Tangerines and Oil–Cured Olives

I'VE BEEN MAKING VARIATIONS on this salad since roasted beets came into vogue a decade ago, and it has survived because it's as easy to make as it is captivating to look at. Like my favorite salads, it's hearty but not heavy, and it features the perfect balance of sweet, salty, and tangy flavors, along with a little crunch from the pepitas (pumpkin seeds). Once you roast the beets, which can be done ahead, this salad comes together in less than 20 minutes.

SERVES 4 · ACTIVE: 20 MIN · TOTAL: 1 HR 15 MIN

2 bunches baby beets in mixed colors, ends trimmed

1 tablespoon extra-virgin olive oil

½ teaspoon fine sea salt

2 tablespoons Sherry-Shallot Vinaigrette (page 286)

½ cup chopped oil-cured olives

1 tablespoon finely sliced fresh chives

1 tablespoon sliced fresh flat-leaf parsley

4 tangerines, peeled and cut into segments (about 2 cups)

Freshly ground black pepper

¼ cup toasted pepitas

Preheat the oven to 350°F.

In a roasting pan, coat the beets in the oil and season with the salt. Cover the pan with aluminum foil and roast the beets for 30 minutes. Remove the foil and continue roasting until the beets are tender in the center when pierced with a paring knife, about 20 more minutes. Let the beets cool, and cut them into bite-size pieces.

In a large bowl, toss the beets with the vinaigrette. Add the olives, chives, parsley, tangerines, four turns of black pepper, and salt to taste. Sprinkle the pepitas on top and serve.

Keep Cool

Success is moving from one failure to another without loss of enthusiasm.
WINSTON CHURCHILL

E very chef I've worked with screws up now and then. It's bound to happen if you cook a lot. I remember Julia Child struggling with a dish during a live demonstration. It was one of the funniest things I've ever seen, and she laughed the hardest.

If your partner gets upset that dinner isn't ready and gives you grief, bag it and have him or her take you out—or have your partner cook dinner next time. If you have guests over and burn the roast, turn it into a blackened, Cajun-style dish, or make it into a rich stew with cream and bold herbs to add moisture and change the flavor. If you like the people you're cooking for and they like you, it's no big deal.

At the Culinary Institute of America, I experienced this firsthand. In a tough class with an intimidating instructor, I was assigned the task of preparing foie gras royale. As I made the custard, I mistakenly lifted my bowl off the base of the food processor, not knowing that it would break the seal keeping the liquid in. I was soon wearing a custard apron. I almost had a heart attack: Not only had I destroyed an expensive ingredient, but I was supposed to be serving it to 80 upperclassmen arriving in 45 minutes. The chef wasn't thrilled, but the show must go on. I ran as fast as I could to the butcher class, grabbed some duck livers, and made it happen. I pulled it off. Barely.

We got a daily grade and performance review at the end of each class in front of our peers. As my turn came up, I was sure of an F. After embarrassing me a little, he announced an A for my quick recovery. Lesson learned: Keep a cool head, be crafty, and make the best out of any challenging situation. ❧

CREAMED SWISS CHARD

with Red Wine Shallots

NO DISRESPECT TO THE classic side dish of creamed spinach, but I happen to think the earthy-sweet flavor and sturdy leaves of Swiss chard are more fitting for the lush treatment. I don't blanch the chard beforehand, so its fresh flavor and texture aren't obscured by the cream.

SERVES 4 TO 6 · ACTIVE: 30 MIN · TOTAL: 30 MIN

2 bunches Swiss chard

4 medium shallots, thinly sliced

½ cup red wine

1 teaspoon sugar

Fine sea salt

2 tablespoons unsalted butter

1 cup heavy cream

2 tablespoons chopped fresh
    tarragon leaves

Finely grated zest of 1 lemon

Freshly ground black pepper

Remove the chard leaves from the ribs and stems. Finely chop the stems and ribs and chop the leaves.

In a small saucepan over low heat, cook half the sliced shallots with the wine, sugar, and a pinch of salt until almost all the wine has evaporated and the sauce is thick and shiny, 2 to 3 minutes.

Melt the butter in a large sauté pan over medium heat. Add the remaining sliced shallots and the chard stems and ribs and cook until they're soft, about 5 minutes. Add the cream, chard leaves, and a pinch of salt and cook, stirring occasionally, until the chard is tender and the cream is reduced enough to coat the chard, 7 to 10 minutes. Stir in the tarragon and lemon zest and season with salt and a few turns of black pepper. Sprinkle the red wine shallots over the top, and serve.

RAINBOW CHARD

with Lentils, Apricots, and Green Curry

SWEET, SPICY, AND EARTHY, this works alongside beef or lamb, or as a satisfying vegetarian meal on its own. Thai green curry paste is an easy find in the Asian section of the grocery store and is one of those pantry items I keep stocked for quick and simple dishes like this one.

SERVES 4 TO 6 · ACTIVE: 20 MIN · TOTAL: 40 MIN

1 large bunch Swiss chard, preferably rainbow chard

1 tablespoon coconut oil

1 large shallot, finely diced

1 tablespoon Thai green curry paste

2 cups cooked lentils, preferably red

½ cup plain yogurt

3 tablespoons diced dried apricots

½ teaspoon fine sea salt

Freshly ground black pepper

Bring a large pot of salted water to a boil.

Pull or cut the large middle stems from the chard leaves. Cut the stems crosswise into ¼-inch-thick pieces and blanch them in the boiling water until tender, about 3 minutes. Pull the stems out of the water with a slotted spoon and drain them in a colander. Bring the water back to a boil and blanch the leaves until tender, about 2 minutes. Drain the leaves and chop coarsely.

In a large saucepan over medium-low heat, melt the coconut oil. Add the shallot and cook until translucent, about 4 minutes. Add the curry paste and cook for 1 minute, constantly stirring so the paste doesn't burn. Add the chard stems and leaves and stir to coat with the curry paste. Stir in the lentils and cook for 3 to 5 minutes, allowing any excess liquid in the pot to evaporate. Reduce the heat to low and fold in the yogurt and apricots. Season with the salt and three turns of black pepper. Serve immediately.

SWISS CHARD PASTILLA

with Smoked Duck and Currants

MY TAKE ON THE classic Moroccan meat pie is a rich, flaky phyllo-wrapped dish of earthy greens contrasted by savory, smoky duck and sweet currants. Tossing in the chard stems adds a little crunch to the filling. Skip the duck for a vegetarian version, or substitute ½ cup crumbled cooked bacon if duck isn't your thing.

SERVES 4 · ACTIVE: 20 MIN · TOTAL: 1 HR

2 tablespoons dried black currants

2 tablespoons red wine, warmed

2 pounds Swiss chard

3 tablespoons extra-virgin olive oil

1 scallion, sliced

1 teaspoon Roasted Garlic Puree (page 77), or ½ teaspoon minced garlic

Fine sea salt

1 cup diced smoked duck breast

2 tablespoons pine nuts

Freshly ground black pepper

6 tablespoons unsalted butter, melted

11 sheets phyllo dough

2 tablespoons dried bread crumbs

Preheat the oven to 350°F. In a small bowl, soak the currants in the wine.

Separate the chard stems from the leaves. Cut the stems into small pieces and the leaves into strips.

In a large skillet, heat the olive oil over high heat. Add the scallion and chard stems and cook for 2 minutes. Add the chard leaves and garlic puree. Season with salt to taste and cook until the chard leaves are tender and any moisture has evaporated, about 5 minutes. Add the wine and currants and cook until the wine has evaporated, about 2 minutes. Stir in the smoked duck and pine nuts. Taste and adjust the seasoning with salt and pepper as needed. Spread the filling out in a baking pan and let it cool.

Generously coat the bottom and sides of an 8-inch ceramic pie plate with melted butter. Brush one side of 5 sheets of phyllo dough with melted butter and arrange them in the dish buttered side down, slightly overlapping each piece and letting the dough hang over the edge by about 6 inches. Brush the phyllo with melted butter and sprinkle 1 tablespoon of the bread crumbs over it. Arrange 5 more sheets of phyllo dough the same way as before. Brush with more melted butter and sprinkle with the remaining 1 tablespoon bread crumbs. Place the last sheet of phyllo dough in the center of the dish.

The filling should be dry at this point, but if there's any liquid, drain it out before pouring the filling into the pie dish. Fold the phyllo dough overhang to cover the filling, so it's completely sealed like a pouch. Brush melted butter on the top.

Bake until the filling is warm and the top is golden brown, about 30 minutes. Let cool for 15 minutes. Put a serving plate on top of the pastilla and flip it over onto the plate, cut into wedges, and serve.

KOHLRABI, APPLE, AND HIJIKI SLAW

I'LL ADMIT THAT THIS combo of ingredients is unusual, but it never fails to be a crowd-pleaser. This slaw is best in the fall, when apples and kohlrabi, a member of the cabbage family, are in season. Serve it with grilled or roasted meats, especially pork, or rich fish like salmon. The tartness of yuzu, a type of Japanese citrus, brings brightness to the slaw and plays well with the umami of the hijiki seaweed. You can find yuzu at Japanese specialty stores and online, or substitute lemon juice for the yuzu.

SERVES 8 · ACTIVE: 20 MIN · TOTAL: 20 MIN

¼ cup dried hijiki seaweed

2 tablespoons rice vinegar

2 tablespoons freshly squeezed yuzu juice or lemon juice

2 tablespoons soy sauce

Finely grated zest of 1 lemon

⅓ cup extra-virgin olive oil

1 pound purple kohlrabi

1 pound apples, preferably Honeycrisp

½ cup sliced fresh basil, preferably Thai basil

3 tablespoons chopped fresh chives

Freshly ground black pepper

Soak the hijiki in 4 cups cold water for 20 minutes. Drain well.

In a large bowl, whisk together the vinegar, yuzu juice, soy sauce, lemon zest, and olive oil.

Remove the stalks and roots from the kohlrabi. Coarsely grate the kohlrabi in a food processor or on the large holes of a box grater. Core the apples and coarsely grate. Add the grated kohlrabi, apples, and hijiki to the bowl with the dressing and toss to coat. Just before serving, toss in the basil, chives, and black pepper to taste. Serve immediately.

TOKYO TURNIPS AND PEARS
with Cardamom Vinaigrette

TOKYO TURNIPS (ALSO KNOWN AS HAKUREI TURNIPS) taste like a cross between a turnip and a radish—tender, juicy, a little sweet, with a bit of spicy sharpness. Look for them at your local farmers' markets from the fall through late spring. Sliced raw and tossed with pears and watercress, they make a crisp, crunchy salad that's great as a side to Blackberry-Basted Pork Tenderloin (page 214) or a rich fish like salmon or black cod.

SERVES 4 · ACTIVE: 20 MIN · TOTAL: 1 HR 20 MIN

2 red Bartlett or Anjou pears

1 tablespoon white wine vinegar, preferably champagne vinegar

1 tablespoon honey

3 tablespoons extra-virgin olive oil

1 teaspoon ground cardamom

¼ teaspoon fine sea salt

Freshly ground black pepper

1 bunch Tokyo or baby white turnips, trimmed and thinly sliced

1 bunch watercress, large stems removed

2 tablespoons chopped fresh chives

1 tablespoon finely grated lemon zest

Core the pears and cut them lengthwise into quarters, then slice into ¼-inch-thick slices. Whisk together the vinegar, honey, oil, cardamom, salt, and one turn of black pepper. Toss the pears and sliced turnips in the vinaigrette to thoroughly coat them. Cover and marinate at room temperature for up to 1 hour.

Just before serving, toss in the watercress, chives, and lemon zest.

ROASTED RUTABAGA

with Grapefruit, Avocado, and Basil

RARELY DO GNARLY-LOOKING RUTABAGAS make it into the grocery basket, let alone shine in a dish, so I like to give the neglected turnip-cabbage hybrid its proper due. Cubes of roasted rutabaga are a deeply savory, yet sweet, earthy contrast to cool, creamy avocado and bright citrus. The variety of textures keeps this exciting bite after bite. It's an excellent snack, but you could serve it with pan-roasted scallops for a light meal.

SERVES 4 AS A SNACK · ACTIVE: 10 MIN · TOTAL: 30 MIN

1 softball-size rutabaga, peeled and cut into ½-inch dice

1 tablespoon extra-virgin olive oil

½ teaspoon fine sea salt

3 ripe red grapefruits, peeled, segmented, and seeded

2 ripe avocados, cut into ½-inch chunks

2 tablespoons roasted unsalted sunflower seeds

¼ cup Coriander-Ginger Vinaigrette (page 288)

5 fresh basil leaves, preferably opal or purple basil

Preheat the oven to 375°F.

On a baking sheet, toss the rutabaga with the olive oil and salt and roast until golden brown and tender, about 20 minutes, stirring every 5 minutes. Allow it to cool to room temperature.

In a bowl, gently toss together the rutabaga, grapefruit, avocado, sunflower seeds, vinaigrette, and basil. Taste and adjust the seasoning as needed. Serve immediately.

CELERY ROOT SALAD

with Pancetta, Walnut Mayonnaise, and Lovage

MAYBE IT'S BECAUSE OF its gnarly exterior or the lack of traffic in farmers' markets in colder months, but celery root (also called celeriac) is one of the most underappreciated vegetables. Its nutty, earthy, subtle celery flavor is surprisingly versatile. Here, it's grated and tossed with a rich walnut mayonnaise for a salad that echoes coleslaw. Lovage, an herb related to parsley, reinforces the celery flavor. If you can't find lovage at your market, use the leaves from the inner stalks of a bunch of celery or flat-leaf parsley instead.

SERVES 4 TO 6 · ACTIVE: 20 MIN · TOTAL: 20 MIN

For the walnut mayonnaise:

1 large egg, at room temperature

2½ tablespoons smooth Dijon mustard

1 teaspoon champagne vinegar or
    white wine vinegar

1 teaspoon soy sauce or tamari, plus more
    if needed

¼ cup walnut oil

½ cup avocado oil

For the salad:

2½ pounds celery root

½ cup crumbled cooked pancetta
    or bacon

¼ cup lovage leaves, sliced

1 cup walnut pieces, finely chopped

2 tablespoons freshly squeezed
    lemon juice

1 teaspoon fine sea salt

Freshly ground black pepper

To make the mayonnaise: Place the egg, mustard, vinegar, and soy sauce in a blender and blend for 1 minute. With the blender running, slowly pour in the walnut oil. Stop to scrape down the sides. With the blender running again, pour in the avocado oil in a slow, steady stream. Taste and add more soy sauce if needed. Reserve 1 cup for the salad and refrigerate the remaining mayonnaise for up to 3 days.

To peel the celery root, cut off the top and the root end. Place the flat, root side down on the cutting board so you have a steady base. Starting from the top, slice the brown skin off in strips, working around the root until clean. Coarsely grate the celery root with a box grater or in a food processor using a coarse grating blade. Immediately toss the grated celery root with the mayonnaise in a large bowl. The celery root will turn brown, so act fast. Add the pancetta, lovage, walnut pieces, lemon juice, salt, and two turns of black pepper. Toss to combine. Taste and adjust the seasoning as needed. Serve immediately, or refrigerate and serve within 24 hours.

The Final Step

Small adjustments can make an average meal amazing.

The recipe is finished and the food you worked so hard on is ready to be served. Don't skip the most important final step: finishing the dish. Take a moment. Taste the dish. Evaluate it. Does it need more salt or pepper? Is the consistency of the soup right? Is the dish balanced? Does it look delicious?

Even time-tested recipes will vary each time you make them. Anyone who has cooked a meal knows that hectic feeling right before serving it; most home cooks fail in the last few minutes. I have seen home cooks come so close to serving a great meal and then drop the ball right before the slam-dunk. Finishing separates the ordinary from the extraordinary. Here are a few crucial elements to pay attention to.

TASTE

SALINITY: Salt is added to food to enhance the ingredients' flavors, not to overpower them. Checking the salt before serving is a must, but don't overdo it.

ACIDITY: Adding a few drops of a quality vinegar or citrus juice brightens up a flat-tasting dish. A little acid perks up everything from soups and salads to fish and roasted meats.

SWEETNESS: Sweetness tempers spicy or tart ingredients and can enhance the natural flavors of fruits and vegetables. I like using a few drops of high-quality artisanal honey, adding floral acacia honey to lighter dishes and bold buckwheat honey to complement full-flavored ones.

AROMA

Add fragrant aromas and flavors with fresh herbs, citrus zests, and finishing oils. Three common aromatic ingredients I turn to most often when finishing a dish are finely grated lemon zest for bright tones, finely sliced chives or scallions for a rustic onion component, and flat-leaf parsley for vegetal flavor.

Every herb has its own nuances. Delicate herbs like chervil, tarragon, and dill pair well with lighter dishes like fish, poultry, and warm weather vegetables. Cilantro, basil, lemon thyme, and mint are fragrant herbs that work well with ethnic flavors and festive food. Bold herbs like thyme, sage, and rosemary can stand up to roasted and seared ingredients and the deep, earthy flavors of fall and winter, like beets, fall squashes, and game meats.

CELERY ROOT SOUP

Fragrant oils are another quick way to add a layer of flavor. High-quality extra-virgin olive oil can add peppery, fruity, and vegetal aromas, and tree nut oils add deep, earthy low tones to dishes (see Choosing Cooking Oils, page 278).

TEXTURE

Your tongue is sensitive to texture, and the combination of contrasting textures makes eating a more delightful experience. Adding a light crunch with a garnish of chopped nuts, finely diced raw vegetables, croutons, or seeds is a simple way to create textural contrast and enhance your presentation.

TEMPERATURE

Variations in temperature add interest. Think of warm pie with ice cream, and take that idea and run with it. Garnish a cold soup with a hot, crunchy ingredient like a fried oyster or a bit of roasted vegetable. A cold dollop of seasoned crème fraîche or sour cream dropped into a hot soup adds a refreshing richness. ❧

CELERY ROOT SOUP

with Trout, Pear, and Curry Oil

THIS SOUP'S EARTHY CELERY root base is satisfying with just a drizzle of olive oil and a side of crusty bread, but I like it best with smoked trout, curry oil, and crunchy pears.

SERVES 6 TO 8 · ACTIVE: 30 MIN · TOTAL: 45 MIN

4 tablespoons unsalted butter

1 large celery root, peeled and cut into ½-inch pieces (about 4 cups)

2 large shallots, diced

1 garlic clove, sliced

¼ cup dry white wine

4 cups Vegetable Stock (page 292)

1 bay leaf

Fine sea salt and freshly ground white pepper

3 tablespoons extra-virgin olive oil

1 teaspoon curry powder

1 slightly underripe Bosc or Anjou pear, cut into matchsticks (about 2 cups)

1 tablespoon apple cider vinegar

8 ounces smoked trout, cleaned, shredded into bite-size pieces

1 tablespoon chopped fresh flat-leaf parsley

1 tablespoon chopped fresh chives

In a large pot, melt the butter over medium-low heat. Add the celery root, shallots, and garlic and cook, stirring occasionally, for 20 minutes. If the vegetables start to brown, reduce the heat to low.

Add the wine and cook until it has almost completely reduced, about 5 minutes. Add the stock, bay leaf, ¼ teaspoon salt, and two turns of black pepper. Increase the heat to medium and cook at a gentle simmer until the celery root is soft and tender, about 30 minutes.

While the soup is simmering, whisk together 1 tablespoon of the olive oil with the curry powder and a pinch of salt in a small bowl. Set aside for at least 20 minutes, so the curry infuses the oil.

In a medium bowl, combine the pear with the vinegar and the remaining 2 tablespoons olive oil. Gently mix in the trout, parsley, and chives, keeping the trout in nice, flaky pieces.

Working in batches if necessary, puree the celery root mixture in a blender until smooth and creamy. Return to the pot over medium heat and taste and adjust the seasoning as needed.

Ladle the hot soup into individual soup bowls. Float some of the trout and pear salad on top. Drizzle the curry oil around the trout salad and serve.

CELERY ROOT AND POTATO GRATIN
with Fresh Horseradish

CONSIDER ADDING THIS DECADENT gratin to your holiday menu, where its richness will be fully appreciated. Celery root is a natural in gratins—it's firm enough to slice thinly and flavorful enough to stand up to a thick blanket of cheese and cream. I like grating fresh horseradish over this because it plays well with the celery flavor (a pairing you probably know well from Bloody Marys). Feel free to be liberal with the fresh horseradish, as it can be milder than the prepared stuff in a jar. Grate a piece of fresh horseradish tableside for a little finishing flourish.

SERVES 6 TO 10 · ACTIVE: 30 MIN · TOTAL: 1 HR 30 MIN

2½ cups heavy cream

1 garlic clove, minced

½ teaspoon celery salt

2 thyme sprigs, plus 4 teaspoons chopped fresh thyme leaves

1 pound celery root

1 pound large russet potatoes

Freshly ground black pepper

½ cup freshly grated Parmigiano-Reggiano

2-inch knob of fresh horseradish, peeled

¼ cup loosely packed fresh flat-leaf parsley, sliced

In a large saucepan over low heat, bring the cream, garlic, celery salt, and thyme sprigs to a low simmer.

Meanwhile, peel the celery root and cut crosswise into ¼-inch slices using a mandoline or a food processor with the slicing attachment. Add the sliced celery root to the simmering cream and turn off the heat. Peel and slice the potatoes into ¼-inch slices.

Position a rack in the center of the oven and preheat the oven to 325°F.

Remove the thyme sprigs from the cream. In a 7 x 9-inch glass or enamel baking dish, spoon enough cream to coat the bottom. Layer one-third of the potato slices evenly in the dish, overlapping them like roof shingles. Spoon one-quarter of the cream on top and layer one-third of the celery root slices in the same way as the potatoes. Sprinkle 1 teaspoon of the chopped thyme, a few turns of black pepper, and 2 tablespoons of the cheese evenly over the celery root layer. Repeat the layers two more times. Pour any leftover cream over the top. For the final layer, sprinkle the remaining 2 tablespoons cheese and 1 teaspoon thyme leaves on top.

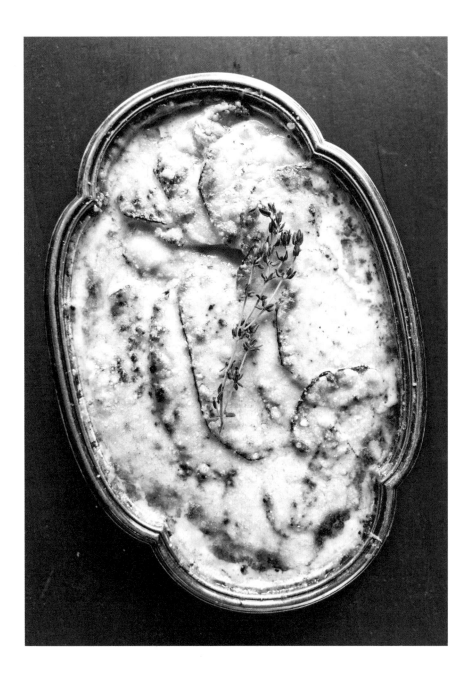

Bake until the top is golden brown and a cake taster or toothpick easily slides into the vegetables, about 45 minutes. Let rest in a warm place for 20 minutes. To serve, grate fresh horseradish and scatter the parsley over the top.

ROASTED SUNCHOKES

with Watercress and Hazelnuts

ROASTING UNPEELED SUNCHOKES LEADS to a satisfying contrast in texture between the earthy roughness of the peel and the soft, sweet centers. Sunchokes have a lot of little nooks and crannies, so give them a good scrub before cooking.

SERVES 4 TO 6 · ACTIVE: 20 MIN · TOTAL: 45 MIN

2 pounds sunchokes, sliced into
¼-inch disks

3½ tablespoons extra-virgin olive oil

Fine sea salt

1 teaspoon balsamic vinegar

Zest and juice of ½ lemon

1½ tablespoons hazelnut oil

1 cup hazelnuts, toasted, skinned,
and crushed

1 bunch watercress, large stems removed

1 tablespoon fresh chives cut into
¼-inch pieces

Preheat the oven to 350°F.

In a roasting pan, toss the sunchokes with 2 tablespoons of the olive oil and ¼ teaspoon salt. Roast until the sunchokes are almost tender with a slight crunch, about 25 minutes, stirring occasionally.

In a large serving bowl, whisk together the vinegar, lemon zest and juice, and a pinch of salt. Whisk in the hazelnut oil and remaining 1½ tablespoons olive oil. Add the hazelnuts and sunchokes and toss. Add the watercress and chives and gently toss again. Taste and adjust the seasoning as needed, and serve immediately.

SUNCHOKE-ALMOND SOUP

WHEN THE WINTER PRODUCE selection seems bleak and boring, try sunchokes (also called Jerusalem artichokes). These tubers create creamy, silky, rich soups—no butter or cream needed. Underneath their knobby exteriors is sweet and nutty flesh that's similar to a potato in texture, and just as versatile. This soup is best topped with a zing of acid, here provided by the pickled oysters.

SERVES 4 · ACTIVE: 35 MIN · TOTAL: 1 HR

1 pound sunchokes

2 tablespoons extra-virgin olive oil

1 shallot, thinly sliced (about 1 tablespoon)

1 garlic clove, chopped

2 teaspoons orange blossom honey

3 cups Vegetable Stock (page 292)

2 thyme sprigs

1 bay leaf

½ teaspoon fine sea salt

Freshly ground black pepper

3 cups unsweetened almond milk, plus more if needed

1 tablespoon almond oil or extra-virgin olive oil

2 tablespoons chopped roasted almonds

4 Pickled Oysters (page 161; optional)

Trim the roots and stems from the sunchokes and cut into 1-inch pieces.

Heat the olive oil in a 4-quart pot over medium-low heat. Add the sunchokes and cook for 5 minutes, stirring occasionally. Add the shallot and garlic and cook until the shallots are translucent, about 3 minutes. Add the honey and cook until it starts to caramelize, about 2 minutes.

Add the vegetable stock, thyme, bay leaf, salt, and two turns of black pepper and cook until the sunchokes are tender, about 25 minutes. Pour in the almond milk and bring to a low simmer. Remove the pot from the stove.

Working in batches, fill a blender about one-third full with soup and puree until smooth. Return the pureed soup to a pot over medium heat to warm it. Adjust the consistency with additional almond milk, if necessary. Season with salt and pepper to taste.

Divide the soup among warm bowls and garnish each with a drizzle of almond oil, a sprinkle of chopped almonds, and a pickled oyster.

CRUSHED YUKON GOLD POTATOES
with Garlic and Parsley

CHEFS OFTEN TREAT POTATOES like a blank canvas for other flavors, but this recipe celebrates how much flavor potatoes have on their own—especially when they're hand-crushed, with their skins on. Olive oil adds a silky richness to the potatoes, but it's mostly here for flavor, so go with a high-quality, peppery variety, and pair this dish with a rich meat like Dry-Rubbed Porterhouse with Tamarind Steak Sauce (page 223).

SERVES 4 TO 6 · ACTIVE: 20 MIN · TOTAL: 1 HR

2 pounds small Yukon Gold potatoes

Fine sea salt

3 tablespoons extra-virgin olive oil

2 to 4 tablespoons Roasted Garlic Puree (page 77), or 1 tablespoon minced garlic

1 cup lightly packed fresh flat-leaf parsley

½ tablespoon fresh thyme leaves

Freshly ground black pepper

Place the potatoes in a large pot and cover with cold water by 3 inches. Add 2 tablespoons salt and bring the water to a simmer over medium heat. Simmer uncovered until the potatoes are tender, 30 to 40 minutes. Drain the potatoes.

In a large bowl or serving dish, combine the potatoes, olive oil, desired amount of garlic puree, ¾ cup of the parsley, the thyme, ½ teaspoon salt, and four turns of black pepper. Crush the potatoes into bite-size pieces with a potato masher or large metal spoon. Toss to combine. Taste and adjust the seasoning as needed, and garnish with the remaining ¼ cup parsley. Serve warm.

POTATOES DAUPHINE
with Scallions and Manchego

THIS DISH TAKES SIMPLE mashed potatoes to a new level. Yes, it adds a few steps, but it's well worth it: By mixing the potatoes with savory pâte à choux (a simple dough that adds air and richness) and frying, they become utterly addictive golden potato nuggets with crispy exteriors and light-as-air interiors. This is a great way to turn leftover potatoes into something spectacular.

SERVES 6 · ACTIVE: 30 MIN · TOTAL: 1 HR 20 MIN

1 pound russet or fingerling potatoes	3 large eggs
Fine sea salt	1 cup grated aged Manchego cheese
6 tablespoons unsalted butter, cut into small pieces	4 scallions, sliced
	Freshly ground black pepper
1 cup all-purpose flour	8 cups vegetable oil

In a medium pot, cover the potatoes with water by 2 inches. Add ¼ teaspoon salt and bring to a simmer over medium-high heat. Cook until the potatoes are tender, about 45 minutes. Drain, peel, and mash the potatoes until smooth.

In another medium pot, bring ¾ cup water and the butter to a simmer over medium-high heat.

Add the flour, reduce the heat to low, and stir continuously until a paste forms and it doesn't stick to the pot, about 2 minutes. Remove from the heat and add the eggs one at a time, beating each one into the dough before adding the next. Add the mashed potatoes and stir in the cheese, scallions, ½ teaspoon salt, and four turns of black pepper.

In a large deep pot, heat the oil to 325°F. Working with one-third of the batter at a time, carefully drop tablespoon-size dollops of batter into the hot oil. Fry until dark golden brown, 4 to 6 minutes. Using a metal slotted spoon, transfer the potatoes to a paper towel–lined plate to drain any excess oil. Fry the remaining batter in the same way. Serve hot.

GREEN GODDESS POTATO SALAD

GREEN GODDESS IS A creamy, no-cooking-required sauce that wears a lot of hats—it's a salad dressing, a dip, and a quick, easy way to liven up vegetables or fish. I like it with a variety of boiled potatoes. Fingerlings, purple Peruvian, and red new potatoes make for a great mix, but you can use any combination you like. In the spring, trade the chives or scallions for ¼ cup sautéed chopped ramps.

SERVES 4 · ACTIVE: 15 MIN · TOTAL: 45 MIN

2 pounds small potatoes, preferably a
    mix of varieties
Fine sea salt
½ cup plain full-fat Greek yogurt
½ cup sour cream
2 tablespoons extra-virgin olive oil

½ cup chopped fresh flat-leaf parsley
¼ cup chopped fresh dill
¼ cup chopped fresh chives or scallions
Finely grated zest and juice of 1 lemon
Freshly ground black pepper

In a large pot, cover the potatoes by at least 1 inch with cold water, and add salt to the water. Bring to a simmer over high heat. Reduce the heat and simmer until a paring knife pokes into the potatoes with little resistance. Start checking after 20 minutes. If using different varieties of potatoes, keep in mind that some may take longer than others to cook. Drain and cut any large potatoes into bite-size pieces.

In a large bowl, stir together the yogurt, sour cream, olive oil, parsley, dill, chives, lemon zest and juice, and salt and pepper to taste. Toss in the warm potatoes and let sit for 5 minutes. Taste and adjust the seasoning as needed, and serve, or let cool and store in an airtight container in the refrigerator for up to 5 days.

PART TWO

SEAFOOD

ROASTED OYSTERS

with Celery, Bacon, and Fresh Horseradish

EVEN IN AN OYSTER-CRAZY city like New York, most people have only experienced them fried or on the half shell. If that's true for you, roasted oysters will be a revelation. Roasting plumps up oysters and brings out their meaty quality without losing any fresh, briny sea flavor. Beausoleil oysters are my top pick because they have a deep cup and meaty texture, but a rich, fat variety like Kumamoto is great too. If you have trouble shucking the oysters, roast them for about 5 minutes, and they'll pop open.

SERVES 4 · ACTIVE: 15 MIN · TOTAL: 30 MIN

4 slices bacon, preferably heritage breed, finely chopped

3 tablespoons finely chopped celery

¼ cup heavy cream

2 tablespoons freshly grated horseradish

Freshly ground black pepper

12 oysters

2 cups coarse salt

Preheat the oven to 350°F.

In a sauté pan over medium heat, brown the chopped bacon until crispy. Add the celery and cook for another minute. Add the cream and horseradish and reduce by half, about 2 minutes. Add two turns of black pepper.

Shuck the oysters, keeping the oyster in the shell. Be sure to cut the bottom muscle to completely release the oyster.

Arrange the salt in an even layer in a baking dish (it will also be the serving dish). Nestle the oysters in their bottom shells (the cup shells) on the salt. Remove the top shells and spoon about a teaspoon of the bacon mixture in each oyster. Place the top shells back on. Bake the oysters until they are plump and the filling is warm, 10 to 15 minutes. Serve immediately.

PICKLED OYSTERS

THESE CAN BE EATEN a handful of ways: as a topping for soup (see Sunchoke-Almond Soup, page 148), on toasted brioche with a dollop of crème fraîche, served with a few toothpicks for a simple bar snack, or dropped into a Bloody Mary or oyster shooter.

SERVES 3 OR 4 · ACTIVE: 20 MIN · TOTAL: 40 MIN

12 medium oysters, shucked, with
    liquid reserved

2 teaspoons champagne vinegar or other
    white wine vinegar

2 tablespoons minced shallot

3 thyme sprigs

2 whole allspice berries

1 whole clove

Pinch of red pepper flakes

Freshly ground black pepper

Strain the liquid from the oysters through a fine-mesh strainer set over a bowl.

Place the oysters and their liquid in a small pot over low heat. When the oysters plump up and their lips begin to slightly curl, 3 to 5 minutes, remove them with a slotted spoon and set aside in a glass or nonreactive bowl.

Add the vinegar, shallot, thyme, allspice, clove, red pepper flakes, four turns of black pepper, and ¼ cup water to the pot of oyster liquid. Bring to a boil over medium heat. Take the pot off the heat and let the liquid cool for 5 minutes. Pour the liquid over the oysters and immediately chill uncovered in the refrigerator for at least 20 minutes. Serve cold, or cover and refrigerate for up to 5 days.

THREE OYSTER SAUCES

EACH OF THESE SAUCES is a lively accompaniment to the salty brininess of oysters, with completely different flavors. My take on a traditional mignonette is light and bright, relying on the minty, anise flavor of perilla, also called shiso leaf. The cayenne pepper sauce is a straightforward fiery flavor. And if you're after a trumped-up version of tartar sauce, head straight for the remoulade.

PERILLA MIGNONETTE

MAKES 1 CUP · ACTIVE: 5 MIN · TOTAL: 5 MIN, PLUS OVERNIGHT

½ cup rice vinegar

2 tablespoons minced shallot

½ teaspoon freshly cracked black pepper

2 perilla (shiso) leaves, thinly sliced

Mix all of the ingredients together in a small bowl, cover, and refrigerate overnight before using. It will keep for up to 2 weeks in the refrigerator.

CAYENNE PEPPER SAUCE

MAKES 1 CUP · ACTIVE: 5 MIN · TOTAL: 5 MIN

6 fresh cayenne chiles, stems removed

1 garlic clove, peeled

¼ teaspoon fine sea salt

¼ cup white wine vinegar

In a blender, blend all of the ingredients together until smooth. Pour through a fine-mesh strainer. Serve right away, or store in an airtight container in the refrigerator for up to 1 month. Shake it up before serving.

PEPPERONCINI-CAPER REMOULADE

MAKES 1 CUP · ACTIVE: 5 MIN · TOTAL: 5 MIN

1 large egg

2 teaspoons freshly squeezed lemon juice

1 cup vegetable oil

1 teaspoon finely grated lemon zest

1 small pepperoncini pepper

1 teaspoon capers, rinsed and drained

1 tablespoon sliced fresh flat-leaf parsley

In a blender, blend the egg and lemon juice for 1 minute on medium speed. Add the oil starting with a few drops, then pouring in a slow, steady stream to create a mayonnaise. Add the zest, pepperoncini, capers, and parsley, and blend until slightly chunky and combined. Serve right away, or store in an airtight container in the refrigerator for up to 2 days.

Where You Are

Everybody needs beauty as well as bread, places to play in and pray in, where
Nature may heal and cheer and give strength to body and soul.

JOHN MUIR

It's hard to enjoy a meal if you're in a bad mood. Your environment influences your mood and behavior. Sound and setting influence the pleasures of eating. The vibe of your dining environment can enhance or dull your tasting experience, so consider *where* you're eating along with *what* you're eating.

Heston Blumenthal, chef of the famed restaurant The Fat Duck in England, performed a fascinating experiment with music. He found that oysters served with a soundtrack of the sea were perceived as more satisfying than oysters served with barnyard sounds. I can't say that barnyard sounds would be appetizing no matter what is on my plate, but it makes sense that when hosting a pool party, the Beach Boys are a better fit than death metal. Try eating pizza while listening to opera, or a 10-course tasting menu while listening to Creedence Clearwater Revival—that would be an interesting experiment.

One of the most memorable meals I can recall was a simple leg of lamb roasted on an open fire at the edge of the pasturelands where the lamb was raised. A lobster roll on a dock in Maine on a sunny summer day will always trump a lobster roll in a concrete stadium or a fancy restaurant.

Being around nature has a positive effect on our well-being. I also believe it influences taste. That can be as simple as fresh flowers on the table, or as impressive as a stunning view overlooking the ocean. A wholesome meal has the power to heal.

Successful restaurants spend a lot of time and money getting their atmosphere just right. Your meal is about more than what is on your plate. Do what you can to enhance the space you're serving it in, and you'll enjoy it more. ❧

SAUTÉED SHRIMP

with Harissa Broth

HARISSA IS A NORTH African chile paste that packs a punch of potent heat. Its spiciness varies depending on the brand, so taste a little before cooking. You won't need much harissa to create a spicy, aromatic broth that pairs well with the sweet, mild flavor of shrimp. Served over polenta, this becomes an exotic version of shrimp and grits.

SERVES 4 · ACTIVE: 35 MIN · TOTAL: I HR

2 tablespoons coconut oil

1 pound large shrimp, preferably Gulf shrimp, peeled and deveined, shells reserved to make the broth

1 medium shallot, diced

2 garlic cloves, coarsely chopped

1 tablespoon harissa

1 lemongrass stalk, coarsely chopped (optional)

¼ cup dry vermouth

2 cups Vegetable Stock (page 292)

Fine sea salt and freshly ground black pepper

½ cup chopped tomatoes

¼ cup fresh cilantro leaves

In a large skillet, heat 1 tablespoon of the oil over high heat until a shrimp shell sizzles immediately when added to the pan. Add the shrimp shells and cook, stirring frequently, until the shells become bright red, about 3 minutes.

Add the shallot and garlic and cook for 1 minute without browning. Add the harissa and lemongrass, if using, and stir frequently for 1 minute. Stir in the vermouth, loosening any brown bits stuck to the bottom of the pan.

Pour in the vegetable stock, reduce the heat to medium-low, and simmer until the liquid reduces by half, about 20 minutes. Remove from the heat and pour the broth through a fine-mesh strainer set over a bowl.

Wipe out the skillet thoroughly. Season the shrimp with salt and pepper. Heat the remaining 1 tablespoon oil in the skillet over medium-high heat until the surface shimmers. Cooking in batches if necessary, add the shrimp to the pan with at least ½ inch space between them. Cook for 2 minutes, then flip and continue cooking until the shrimp is almost completely white, another 2 to 3 minutes.

Reduce the heat to low. Add the tomatoes, cilantro, and harissa broth to the skillet. Heat for about 3 minutes to allow the flavors to come together, and serve.

CHINATOWN SHRIMP

DUMPLINGS AND NOODLES MAY be the main attractions at most Chinese restaurants, but when I head to Brooklyn's Chinatown in Sunset Park, I'm all about the shrimp dishes. This has a little something from all of my favorites—shrimp tempura, shrimp with cashews, coconut shrimp, and salt-and-pepper shrimp.

SERVES 4 · ACTIVE: 10 MIN · TOTAL: 20 MIN

1 cup crushed raw cashews

1 cup raw coconut flakes

½ cup all-purpose flour

1 tablespoon cornstarch

½ teaspoon baking powder

1 teaspoon garlic salt

1 teaspoon ground coriander

½ teaspoon sweet paprika

½ teaspoon freshly ground black pepper

1 cup vegetable oil

1 pound large tail-on shrimp, preferably Gulf shrimp, peeled and deveined, tails left on

½ head iceberg lettuce or napa cabbage, chopped

½ cup cilantro sprigs

Spicy Honey-Lime Sauce (page 171), for serving

In a medium bowl, toss the cashews and coconut together. In another medium bowl, combine the flour, cornstarch, baking powder, garlic salt, coriander, paprika, and pepper.

Make a well in the center of the flour mixture and slowly pour ½ cup cold water into the well, whisking from the center of the bowl and gradually moving out toward the sides to incorporate the flour. Whisk until smooth.

In a 10-inch skillet, heat the oil to 325°F. Dredge the shrimp in the batter to coat evenly. Remove the shrimp using tongs or chopsticks and shake off any excess batter. Dredge the shrimp one at a time in the cashew mixture until completely coated.

Working in batches of 4 or 5 shrimp at a time, slowly lower the shrimp into the pan with metal tongs. Fry for 3 minutes, then flip and fry for another 3 minutes, or until the batter is golden brown on both sides. Using a slotted metal spoon, transfer the shrimp to a paper towel–lined plate. Make sure the oil is at 325°F before frying the next batch.

Arrange the lettuce on a serving platter. Place the fried shrimp on the bed of lettuce, scatter the cilantro sprigs on top, and serve with honey-lime sauce.

SHRIMP AND KIMCHI FRITTERS

I CAN'T GET ENOUGH of *kimchi jeon*, savory Korean pancakes made with little more than spicy kimchi (fermented cabbage), flour, and egg. To make them more of a main course, I add shrimp and a shower of fresh herbs to the batter, and serve them with a sweet, peppy dipping sauce. They turn out crispy, a bit chewy, and full of umami and spicy zing from the kimchi. Thanks to the resurgence of fermented vegetables, there are more brands of kimchi available than ever before, from small-batch Brooklyn-based brands (my favorite) to the traditional versions sold at Korean specialty stores.

SERVES 4 (MAKES ABOUT 8 FRITTERS) · ACTIVE: 10 MIN · TOTAL: 30 MIN

8 ounces fresh large shrimp, preferably Gulf shrimp, peeled and deveined and cut into small pieces

2 cups kimchi, drained and coarsely chopped (reserve the liquid for the Spicy Honey-Lime Sauce)

1 cup all-purpose flour

½ cup rice flour

6 scallions, finely chopped

2 tablespoons chopped fresh cilantro

2 tablespoons chopped fresh basil, preferably Thai basil

½ teaspoon fine sea salt

Freshly ground black pepper

Dash of fish sauce

1 large egg, lightly beaten

½ cup avocado oil

Spicy Honey-Lime Sauce (recipe follows), for serving

In a large bowl, mix together the shrimp, kimchi, both flours, the scallions, cilantro, basil, salt, and four turns of black pepper. Add the fish sauce, egg, and 1 cup cold water, and stir until the batter is smooth. Let sit for 15 minutes.

Heat 1 to 2 tablespoons of the oil in a large sauté pan over medium heat. Working in batches of 2 fritters at a time, spoon in 2 tablespoons of the shrimp mixture per fritter. Flatten to about ½ inch thick and cook until brown, crispy, and firm in the center, 2 to 3 minutes on each side. Transfer the fritters to a paper towel–lined plate to drain. Repeat with the remaining shrimp mixture, wiping out the skillet and heating fresh oil between batches if the oil becomes dark. Serve the fritters with honey-lime sauce for dipping.

SPICY HONEY-LIME SAUCE

MAKES ABOUT ½ CUP

2 tablespoons reserved kimchi liquid

1 tablespoon honey

1 tablespoon freshly squeezed lime juice

1 tablespoon extra-virgin olive oil

1 tablespoon soy sauce

Pinch of red pepper flakes

Whisk all of the ingredients together in a bowl. Refrigerate in an airtight container for up to 1 week.

STOVE-SMOKED SCALLOPS AND MUSSELS
with Pasta

SMOKING SEAFOOD ON THE stovetop may seem intimidating, but all you need is a stockpot, a steamer insert, and some aluminum foil and you are ready to start smoking. The exotic, lightly smoked scallops and mussels add a subtle twist to an otherwise straightforward fresh tomato linguine. I prefer sustainably farm-raised Prince Edward Island mussels. In many cases, sustainably farmed seafood can be a better environmental choice than buying overfished local varieties.

SERVES 4 · ACTIVE: 30 MIN · TOTAL: 30 MIN

1 cup turbinado sugar

3 whole star anise

2 tablespoons coriander seeds

1½ pounds mussels, preferably from Prince Edward Island, scrubbed and debearded

1 pound medium scallops, patted dry

2 tablespoons unsalted butter

2 shallots, thinly sliced

2 tablespoons dry white wine

1 pound linguine (or other long pasta), cooked al dente

Fine sea salt and freshly ground black pepper

1 cup diced tomatoes, preferably heirloom

2 tablespoons fresh flat-leaf parsley leaves

4 fresh basil leaves, sliced

Prepare a stovetop smoker by lining the bottom of a large stockpot with aluminum foil. Combine the sugar, star anise, and coriander seeds and sprinkle the mixture in the pot. Put the mussels and scallops in a folding metal steamer insert and place it in the pot. Turn the heat to high and cover with a tight lid when it starts to smoke. If smoke is still escaping, seal the top with aluminum foil, then replace the lid. Reduce the heat to medium-low and smoke the mussels and scallops for 6 minutes. Turn off the heat and let sit covered for 10 minutes. Remove the mussels from their shells and discard any mussels that didn't open.

In a large skillet over low heat, melt the butter. Add the shallots and wine and cook until the shallots are translucent, about 2 minutes. Toss the pasta in the sauce and season with salt and pepper to taste. Cook for a couple of minutes. Then toss in the tomatoes, parsley, mussels, and scallops. Cook for a couple of minutes to allow everything to come together. Sprinkle with the basil just before serving.

SEARED SCALLOPS

with Roasted Cauliflower and Olive Puree

SEARED SCALLOPS ARE SO sweet and tender that they don't need much else to make a beautiful dish. Roasted cauliflower complements their richness, and a simple olive puree adds a nice brininess. If blood oranges or grapefruit are in season, a cup of segments tossed with the pea shoots brings a bright, juicy pop to the dish.

SERVES 4 · ACTIVE: 20 MIN · TOTAL: 30 MIN

2 heads cauliflower, cut into 1-inch florets (about 8 cups)

2 tablespoons extra-virgin olive oil, plus more for serving

Fine sea salt

½ cup pitted black olives, preferably Kalamata or Alfonso

½ cup Vegetable Stock (page 292) or water

Finely grated zest and juice of 1 lemon

¼ cup fresh basil leaves, sliced

2 tablespoons avocado or coconut oil

1½ pounds jumbo scallops (12 to 16 scallops)

Freshly ground black pepper

4 ounces young pea shoots

Preheat the oven to 375°F. Place a large roasting pan in the hot oven for 5 minutes.

Toss the cauliflower with the olive oil and ¼ teaspoon salt in a bowl. Pour the cauliflower into the preheated pan in an even layer and roast until golden brown, about 15 minutes, stirring once halfway through roasting.

In a blender, puree the olives, vegetable stock, lemon juice, and half the basil until smooth, about 2 minutes.

Heat the cooking oil in a large skillet over medium-high heat. Pat the scallops dry and season with salt and pepper on both sides. Cooking in batches if necessary, add the scallops to the skillet, leaving at least 1½ inches between each scallop. Sear until golden brown, 3 to 4 minutes per side.

Scatter the pea shoots on a serving platter. Sprinkle the roasted cauliflower over the pea shoots, then lay the scallops on top. Drizzle the olive puree over everything and finish with a sprinkle of lemon zest, the remaining basil, and a drizzle of olive oil.

SCALLOPS MARINATED

with Horseradish and Lemon Thyme

THE ONLY REAL SECRET to this vibrant dish is using the freshest, highest-quality scallops you can find. Ask your fishmonger for large, dry-pack scallops (a label that means they're packaged without additives)—plump, sweet, diver-caught scallops are my top pick. If horseradish isn't your thing, add a little kick of heat in the form of red pepper flakes or paper-thin slices of fresh jalapeño.

SERVES 4 · ACTIVE: 15 MIN · TOTAL: 30 MIN

5 tablespoons extra-virgin olive oil

Finely grated zest and juice of 1 lemon

1 tablespoon finely chopped shallot

1 teaspoon finely chopped fresh lemon thyme leaves

8 large sea scallops (about 1 pound), patted dry

Fine sea salt and freshly ground black pepper

1 bunch watercress, stems removed, or 2 cups nasturtium leaves

2 tablespoons freshly grated horseradish root

Flaky sea salt, for serving

Whisk together the olive oil, lemon juice, shallot, and lemon thyme in a glass bowl. Slice the scallops crosswise into ⅛-inch-thick disks. Gently toss the scallops with the lemon juice mixture and season with ½ teaspoon salt and four turns of black pepper. Cover with plastic wrap or parchment paper and refrigerate for 15 minutes.

Arrange the watercress around the edge of a large plate or platter. Artfully place the scallops in a single layer in the center of the plate, slightly overlapping them. Scatter the horseradish shavings evenly over the scallops, then sprinkle with the lemon zest and a pinch of flaky sea salt. Serve immediately.

Food Matters

Little choices make a big difference.

Cooking is a definitive social experience and personal choice. What we cook and eat is an essential daily decision; how we shop for ingredients expresses a statement of our values. How we choose our food directly affects how it tastes, our personal health, and the health of our communities. When we make food that is healthy for our bodies and environments, by using sustainable ingredients and supporting the communities we live in by buying local, everyone wins.

I understand the counterargument: "This isn't practical. I have a demanding job, children, a tiny kitchen, and no garden. I don't have time to hop on the subway or drive twenty minutes to the farmers' market, make my own vegetable stock, grow my own vegetables. I don't have time to be thinking about everything I put in my mouth." It's a realistic response. We all lead busy lives. But those lives are made better when we stop to consider what we eat and why.

As a chef I feel an obligation to use the "right" products, to highlight great local produce, to support the community. It can feel like I have an overzealous food activist sitting on my shoulder, reminding me, "That's not organic, that's not local, and that's not grass-fed." I have compassion for that voice, but if I listened to it all the time my restaurant would be out of business and I would be living in the woods.

Still, when I get frustrated at the market, waiting in line or dealing with crowds, I try to embrace the idea that the daily choices I make can have a positive impact. Changing your approach to cooking is a simple way to contribute to a greater cause. The sum of your choices has a profound personal effect and improves the quality and enjoyment of your cooking and the world we live in.

The Brooklyn Rustic approach is an effort to balance the little choices we make every day with a larger holistic picture. I selected the main ingredients in this book to leave the choice of this approach up to you. Almost every highlighted ingredient can be found in most modern supermarkets and also at the farmers' market when in season. Even staple items like soy sauce or cooking oil present a choice. Do you buy organic soy sauce for a couple more dollars? Do you use organic cooking oils instead of chemically processed vegetable oils? My choice was made quickly, after I compared the smell and taste of the chemically processed oils to the natural ones.

Awareness and connection can start with the simplest act. Change is driven by us, the consumers and voters, not by producers and politicians. Change can begin with thoughtful choices about how we cook and eat. ❖

BLACK COD

with Figs and Fennel

BLACK COD, ALSO CALLED butterfish or sablefish, is a really rich, dense fish that's hard to overcook. Sweet figs and herbaceous fennel work well together to make an unusual duo. If you can find them, use fresh figs in place of dried—just cut them and toss them into the baking dish when the fish goes in.

SERVES 4 · ACTIVE: 20 MIN · TOTAL: 40 MIN, PLUS 30 MIN TO 4 HR FOR MARINATING

¾ cup freshly squeezed orange juice

2 tablespoons yellow miso

1 tablespoon soy sauce

2½ teaspoons sherry vinegar

¾ cup stemmed and diced dried figs

1 small bunch basil, preferably Thai or cinnamon basil, sliced with stems reserved

4 (4- to 6-ounce) skinless black cod fillets

1 medium fennel bulb

1 small shallot or scallion, thinly sliced

Combine the orange juice, miso, soy sauce, vinegar, and figs in a small saucepan and simmer for 5 minutes. Take out the figs and set them aside. Toss in the basil stems, remove the pot from the stove, and let it sit until it reaches room temperature. Remove and discard the basil stems.

Place the fish in a shallow glass baking dish, pour in the liquid, and marinate, covered in the refrigerator, for at least 30 minutes and up to 4 hours.

Preheat the oven to 400°F.

Remove the stalks and outer tough layer from the fennel. Trim off the bottom of the stem if it's brown. Using a mandoline or sharp knife, cut the fennel into ⅛-inch-thick slices. Put the sliced fennel in the bottom of a nonreactive baking dish and scatter the shallot evenly over the fennel. Arrange the fish on top and pour the marinade over it. Roast for 10 minutes. Scatter the reserved figs around the fish and baste the fish with the marinade. Roast for another 10 minutes, or until the fish is lightly browned and firm to the touch and the fennel is tender. Sprinkle the basil over the fish and serve.

CRAB-CRUSTED HALIBUT

ON A TOUR THROUGH Halifax, Nova Scotia, I visited a sustainable halibut farm that served me an outrageously rich, delicious halibut that was raised on crabmeat for feed. To have a similar taste of that delicacy here at home, I came up with this buttery crab crust. You can use it on any thick white fish—cod, perch, Dover sole, and more. It's a winning dish for a special occasion, and simple enough for a random Tuesday night.

SERVES 4 TO 6 · ACTIVE: 15 MIN · TOTAL: 45 MIN

1 stick (8 tablespoons) unsalted butter, cubed and chilled, plus more to grease the pan

2 cups cubed brioche or challah bread, crust removed

1 cup spinach, stems removed and coarsely chopped

Fine sea salt and black pepper

1 teaspoon finely grated lemon zest

8 ounces fresh peekytoe or lump crabmeat, picked free of shells, drained well (about 1 cup)

4 to 6 (6-ounce) skinless halibut fillets, 1½ inches thick

Cut two large squares of parchment paper (about 12 inches square). Butter a nonstick baking sheet.

In a food processor, spin the bread until it becomes coarse bread crumbs. Add the butter, spinach, ¼ teaspoon salt, and two turns of black pepper, and pulse until just combined. Add the crab and pulse until evenly incorporated and it reaches a smooth, spreadable consistency.

Transfer the crust with a spatula to a piece of the parchment paper. Place the other piece of parchment paper on top of that. With a rolling pin, roll out the crust to about a ¼-inch thickness. Refrigerate until the crust is firm, about 10 minutes.

Meanwhile, preheat the oven to 350°F. Lightly season the halibut all over with salt and pepper and put the fillets on the prepared baking sheet. Cut the crust into pieces about the size of the halibut fillets and lay a piece on each fillet. Bake until the fish is firm and warm in the center and the crust is lightly browned, 10 to 15 minutes. Serve immediately.

CURED SALMON

with Arugula, Beets, and Horseradish-Chive Cream

CURING YOUR OWN SALMON is a two-day process, but you're by no means babysitting it. The majority of the time is spent anticipating all the ways you'll enjoy the soft, silky flesh—piled in sandwiches, served alongside Soft Scrambled Eggs with Chives and Brioche (page 198), shaved into slices for appetizers. To reward myself for my patience, I love to show off the salmon in a bright, beautiful salad like the one here. Once you get the method of curing down, you can fool around with the cure by adding others herbs and seasonings, like dill or basil, mustard seeds, and finely grated citrus zest. The quality of the salmon is the constant here—I use only wild Alaskan or organic farmed salmon, which are the most sustainable and flavorful varieties.

SERVES 4 · ACTIVE: 40 MIN · TOTAL: 2 DAYS

Coarse sea salt

2 tablespoons light brown sugar

1 tablespoon fennel seeds

1 tablespoon coriander seeds

1 tablespoon whole black peppercorns

¼ cup loosely packed fresh lemon verbena, sliced

1 ounce vodka

1½ pounds skin-on wild Alaskan salmon, about 1 inch thick, pin bones removed

¼ cup crème fraîche

2 tablespoons extra-virgin olive oil

1 teaspoon freshly squeezed lemon juice

2 tablespoons finely grated fresh horseradish

2 teaspoons sliced fresh chives

8 ounces arugula

2 cups baby beets (about 1 bunch), roasted and quartered

Freshly ground black pepper

In a blender or food processor, pulse ½ cup salt, the brown sugar, fennel seeds, coriander seeds, and peppercorns until coarsely ground. In a medium bowl, mix the ground spices, lemon verbena, and vodka.

Dry the salmon with a paper towel and place skin side down on a wire rack set over a baking sheet lined with parchment paper. Spread the salt mixture over the top of the salmon. Place another piece of parchment on top of the salted salmon and tightly wrap the entire pan in plastic wrap. Refrigerate for about 48 hours, until the salmon feels firm to the touch. Rinse off the salt with cold water and dry the salmon with paper towels. You may now store the salmon tightly wrapped in the refrigerator for up to 5 days.

In a medium bowl, whisk together the crème fraîche, 1 tablespoon of the olive oil, the lemon juice, horseradish, and 1 teaspoon of the chives until smooth.

Arrange a layer of arugula on a large platter or four individual plates. Thinly slice the salmon crosswise on the bias with a sharp knife, discarding the skin and any gray flesh. Layer the salmon over the arugula, leaving a little green showing on the edge to frame the salmon. Toss the beets in a bowl with the remaining 1 tablespoon olive oil and remaining teaspoon of chives, and season with salt and pepper to taste. Scatter the beets over the salmon and drizzle the horseradish cream over the top.

STRIPED BASS POACHED IN CORN BROTH

THIS IS A LIGHT, hassle-free meal that has the unmistakable taste of summer. Most types of fish take well to poaching in the oven, but this technique is especially suited to the meaty fillets of striped bass. If the fillets are from smaller fish, less than an inch thick, fold them in half to keep the fish as moist and tender as possible. This technique creates a thicker portion that cooks more slowly, which is what you want when poaching. Other white fish, like halibut, black sea bass, or lemon sole, work well here too.

SERVES 6 · ACTIVE: 15 MIN · TOTAL: 35 MIN

6 (6- to 8-ounce) skinless striped bass fillets, pin bones removed

Fine sea salt and freshly ground white pepper

Unsalted butter, for greasing the pan

Leaves from 2 thyme sprigs

Finely grated zest and juice of 1 lemon

2 quarts Corn Broth (page 63), warmed

Preheat the oven to 300°F.

Lightly season the fish with salt and white pepper. Lay each fillet skin side up and fold in half, touching the tail to the top of the fillet. Put the tail side on the bottom. With a sharp knife, cut crosswise, halfway through each fillet where it bends, so the top and bottom of the fillet stay connected but form one thick portion.

Lightly butter a 9 x 13-inch glass baking dish. Place the fish in the baking dish, allowing some space between fillets. Sprinkle the thyme leaves and lemon zest over the fish, and gently pour the warm corn broth and lemon juice over the fish.

Bake for 15 to 20 minutes, ladling the broth over the fish every 5 minutes to keep it moist. The fish is done when it's warm in the center and a cake tester or paring knife can pass through a fillet with no resistance. Divide the fish among bowls and ladle the broth over each as a sauce.

SPRING ONION—STUFFED BROOK TROUT
with Pine Nuts

YOUR FISHMONGER DOES MOST of the work by butterflying the trout, so this recipe is actually quite simple. Pine nuts bring out the sweet, deep taste of cooked trout and offer a nice crunch to contrast with the tender flesh. If you are on a fishing trip, this is great over an open fire with ramps or wild onions and yesterday's bread for the bread crumbs. If you don't have a fish grill basket, tie each fish with wet kitchen twine in three places and cook on the grill or in a sauté pan.

SERVES 4 · ACTIVE: 15 MIN · TOTAL: 30 MIN

1 cup fresh bread crumbs

½ cup pine nuts

¼ cup sliced fresh flat-leaf parsley

1 tablespoon finely grated lemon zest

2 tablespoons plus 1 teaspoon extra-virgin olive oil

Fine sea salt and freshly ground black pepper

4 whole brook trout (or Arctic char), scaled, butterflied, and heads, tails, and fins removed

8 spring onions, scallions, or ramps, ends trimmed

Prepare a hot grill and oil the grill rack.

In a large bowl, toss together the bread crumbs, pine nuts, parsley, lemon zest, 1 tablespoon of the olive oil, 1 teaspoon salt, and 1 teaspoon black pepper.

Rinse the trout and pat dry. Rub 1 teaspoon of the olive oil on the outside of each trout and season with salt and pepper. Place one-quarter of the stuffing in the cavity of each trout, spreading evenly from the head end to the tail end. Lay 2 spring onions in each fish.

Grill the trout in a fish grill basket until the stuffing is hot and the fish is opaque in the center, about 7 minutes on each side.

GRILLED BRANZINO

with Fennel and Olive Escabeche

GREAT GRILLED BRANZINO NEEDS little more than a squeeze of lemon, but dressing it escabeche-style makes it especially refreshing and summery. Instead of marinating the fish before grilling, the acidic dressing goes on afterward, when the branzino is hot and able to drink up more of the bright, salty escabeche. Keeping the skin on the fish is key because it protects the delicate flesh while it grills.

SERVES 4 · ACTIVE: 20 MIN · TOTAL: 30 MIN

½ small fennel bulb, cut lengthwise into ¼-inch wedges

Extra-virgin olive oil

Fine sea salt and freshly ground black pepper

2 tablespoons oil-cured black olives, pitted and finely diced

2 tablespoons diced roasted red bell peppers

1 tablespoon seeded and diced lemon segments

1 tablespoon sliced fresh flat-leaf parsley

1 teaspoon capers, rinsed and finely chopped

4 (6- to 8-ounce) skin-on branzino fillets

Prepare a hot grill and oil the grill rack.

Coat the fennel in a little olive oil and season with salt and pepper to taste. Grill on each side for about 2 minutes, or until you see charred grill marks. Dice the fennel and toss in a bowl with 2 tablespoons of the olive oil, the olives, roasted peppers, lemon, parsley, capers, and two turns of black pepper. Taste and adjust the seasoning if needed.

Pat the fish dry. Lightly brush both sides with olive oil and season with salt and pepper. On a medium-hot area of the grill, cook the fillets skin side down, covered, for 4 to 6 minutes. The flesh should be opaque and firm to the touch. It's okay if the skin gets slightly charred—in fact, that's what you want. Transfer to a serving dish. Spoon the escabeche over the fish and let marinate for 10 minutes. Serve warm.

BLACK SEA BASS

with Pepita Crust

I FIRST MADE THIS dish when I cooked at a Manhattan restaurant called Union Pacific, and I brought it with me to Brooklyn because it's a simple dish that delivers great texture and a lot of flavor. We used sunflower seeds back then, but I prefer the flavor and texture of pepitas (pumpkin seeds), especially in the fall. Leaving the skin on helps to protect the fish from overcooking, and black sea bass in particular has delicate skin that's not too cumbersome to eat. For an easy, light weeknight dinner, look no further.

SERVES 4 · ACTIVE: 15 MIN · TOTAL: 30 MIN

2½ tablespoons extra-virgin olive oil

2 cups raw pepitas

Fine sea salt

2 teaspoons chopped fresh thyme leaves

2 large egg whites

4 (6- to 8-ounce) skin-on black sea bass fillets, pin bones removed

Freshly ground black pepper

1 tablespoon unsalted butter, softened

4 lemon wedges

Heat ½ tablespoon of the olive oil in a large sauté pan over medium heat. Add 1 cup of the pepitas and toss constantly until they puff up a little bit. Season with ¼ teaspoon salt and let cool.

In a food processor, spin the remaining 1 cup of pepitas with 1 teaspoon of the thyme until they become a flour-like powder. Add the cooked pepitas and pulse to chop into a coarse crust. Transfer the pepita mixture to a shallow pan.

Lightly whisk the egg whites with a pinch of salt. Brush the skin side of the bass fillets with the egg to coat the entire skin. Press the skin side of the fillets into the pepita mixture to create a crust.

In a large skillet, heat 1 tablespoon of the olive oil over medium-low heat. Working with 2 fillets at a time, place the fish crust side down in the pan. Season the fish with a little salt and black pepper and cook until the crust turns golden brown, about 5 minutes. Gently turn the fillets over and add ½ tablespoon of the butter and ½ teaspoon of the remaining thyme. Cook until the flesh is opaque and firm, 2 to 3 minutes more. Transfer the fillets to serving plates and squeeze a wedge of lemon over the crust of each one. Repeat this process to cook the remaining 2 fillets. Serve warm.

COD

with Sweet Peppers and Spicy Sausage

THIS IS AN IDEAL dinner for a summer night. It comes together in one skillet, there's nothing finicky or tedious, and it works well with cold, crisp beer and a bunch of friends. It's even better if you can grill the sausages before slicing and adding them to the pan. If you've got the grill going, char the peppers on there as well.

SERVES 4 · ACTIVE: 10 MIN · TOTAL: 20 MIN

3 tablespoons extra-virgin olive oil

2 (4-ounce) spicy pork sausages

2 sweet Italian frying peppers or red bell peppers, cut lengthwise into ¼-inch slices

1 small fresh red Thai chile pepper, sliced in half (or a pinch of red pepper flakes)

1 tablespoon Roasted Garlic Puree (page 77), or 2 teaspoons finely chopped garlic

½ cup Vegetable Stock (page 292)

1 tablespoon rice vinegar

1 tablespoon tamari

4 (6- to 8-ounce) skinless cod fillets

Fine sea salt and freshly ground black pepper

¼ cup thinly sliced spring onion greens or scallions

¼ cup fresh flat-leaf parsley leaves

In a skillet over medium heat, heat 1 tablespoon of the olive oil and cook the sausages for about 5 minutes, until they are firm enough to cut. Cut the sausage into ¼-inch-thick slices.

Heat the remaining 2 tablespoons olive oil in the same skillet over medium heat. Add the sliced sausages, Italian peppers, chile pepper, and garlic puree and cook until the peppers become soft, about 5 minutes. Add the vegetable stock, vinegar, and tamari and give it a stir.

Season the cod fillets with salt and pepper and place on top of the peppers and sausage, leaving at least ½ inch between fillets. Sprinkle the spring onion greens over the fish. Cover with a tight-fitting lid, reduce the heat to medium-low, and cook until the cod becomes white and firm to the touch, about 7 minutes. A skewer or cake tester inserted into the center of a cod fillet should have no resistance and pull out warm. Garnish with the parsley and a few turns of black pepper and serve.

PART THREE

MEAT AND POULTRY

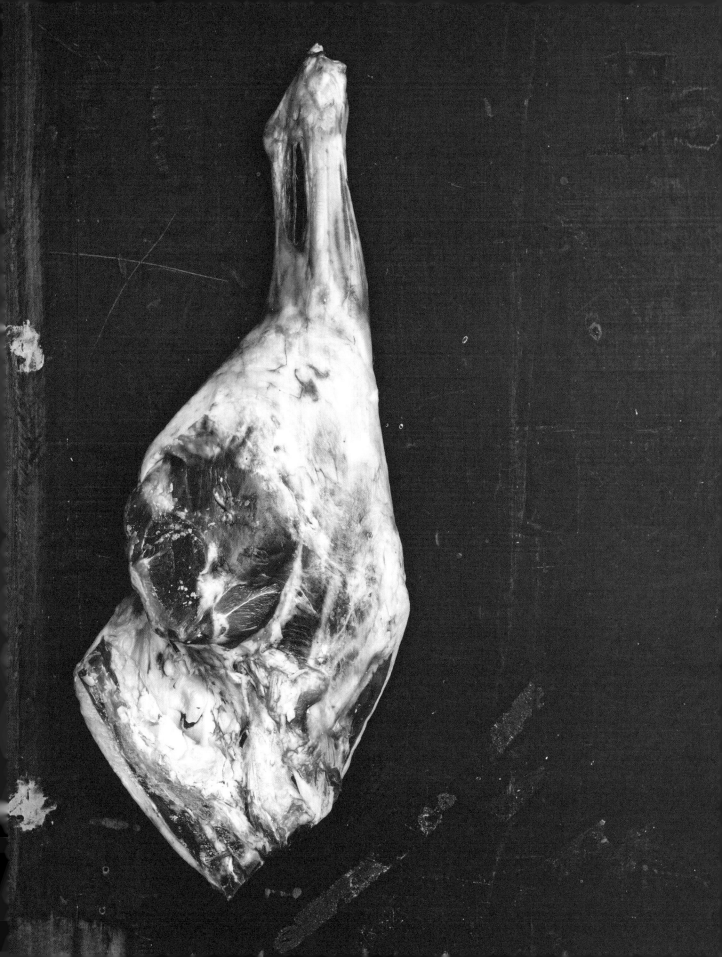

The Power of an Egg

Laying a poached or fried egg over a dish has become fashionable as more people adopt a vegetarian diet or look to incorporate non-meat proteins into their meals. But it's actually an old-world technique with timeless value.

A perfectly cooked egg rounds out lean dishes, elevates last night's vegetable side to the status of tonight's main course, brings luster to an otherwise dull plate, and carries good dishes to greatness. Poached and fried eggs work best as garnishes—one is soft, subtle, and rich, while the other has crunchy edges with a silken center.

Eggs are also an excellent starting point to switch from conventionally produced food to a more sustainable version, which can mean local or organic or both. The labels on eggs can be confusing—organic, cage-free, free-range, pastured, vegetarian. My rule is to buy fresh eggs from the farmers' market and ask the farmer how the chickens are raised and what they are fed. I like to hear that the chickens are pastured or free-range, and, ideally, that they eat organic feed. (Note that many small farmers who use organic practices are not "certified organic" by the USDA—certification is expensive and onerous.) When I can't make it to the farmers' market, I buy certified organic or local eggs in the supermarket. They cost a couple bucks more per dozen but are well worth it for their quality, flavor, and health benefits.

POACHED EGGS

Bring 1 quart of water to a boil. Add a dash of distilled white vinegar. Reduce the heat to a low simmer. Crack the egg into a ramekin, teacup, or small bowl, and then slip it into the simmering water. Without touching the egg, gently stir the water once around the pot, so the egg moves a little and releases from the bottom of the pot. Poach for 1½ minutes at a very low simmer, and remove with a slotted spoon. Scrape away any loose cooked whites. Season with salt and pepper and lay it on top of your dish. The result will be a delicate, warm, slightly viscous liquid yolk encapsulated by a soft, gelatinous white.

If you're poaching a few eggs at once, use more water—2 quarts of water per 4 eggs. If you have a big crew and need a lot of eggs, try getting ahead by poaching batches for 1 minute, cooling them in ice-cold salted water, and then reheating them in the gently simmering water for 30 seconds before serving. I only like to get ahead within an hour of serving.

CRISPY FRIED EGGS

Frying eggs in oil over high heat creates a crunchy texture and caramelization that pair well with strong flavors. Cooking only one side creates a crispy bottom with a soft top—basically a sunny-side-up egg with an extra-crispy bottom. In a seasoned heavy skillet or sauté pan (see Season Your Pots, Pans, and Grill, page 276), heat 1 tablespoon of avocado oil or extra-virgin olive oil over medium heat. I don't suggest using a pan with a nonstick coating; most shouldn't be used for high-heat cooking (see Set Up for Success, page 276). Crack the egg into a small bowl or teacup. When you see the first whiffs of smoke coming off the oil, slide the egg into the center of the pan and fry for 1 minute. Use a thin metal spatula to loosen the egg from the bottom of the pan. Reduce the heat to low and cook for an additional 2 minutes. Season with salt and pepper and lay the egg over your dish. ❧

SOFT SCRAMBLED EGGS

with Chives and Brioche

I PUT SCRAMBLED EGGS high on the list of dishes worth mastering. They are among the simplest, most comforting of foods, quick to put together and infinitely variable. Making the lightest, fluffiest, no-fail scrambled eggs requires a couple of extra steps that you may not be used to: first, beating the eggs in a blender to whip more air into them, and then slow-cooking them in a double boiler over low heat so they cook more evenly. This is a surefire way to perfectly cook a big batch of rich, decadent eggs for a group.

SERVES 4 · ACTIVE: 20 MIN · TOTAL: 20 MIN

8 large eggs

Fine sea salt

1 tablespoon unsalted butter

2 tablespoons crème fraîche or
    sour cream

2 tablespoons thinly sliced fresh chives

Freshly ground black pepper

4 slices Brioche (page 283), buttered
    and toasted

Bring a saucepan of water to a simmer over low heat. Set a large stainless steel bowl over (but not touching) the water.

To thoroughly combine the egg yolks and whites, add them to a blender with a few pinches of salt and blend for about 30 seconds. If you don't have a blender, whisk thoroughly until completed combined and slightly frothy.

Melt the butter in the double boiler. Pour in the eggs and whisk back and forth, starting slowly and whisking faster as the eggs start to thicken. Make sure to whisk the sides and bottom of the bowl so the eggs cook evenly and no skin forms.

Just as the eggs start to thicken into small, soft curds, after about 5 minutes, remove the bowl from the water (watch out for the hot water dripping from the underside of the bowl). Whisk in the crème fraîche, chives, ½ teaspoon salt, and two turns of black pepper. Serve immediately with the buttered toasted brioche.

DEVILED EGGS THREE WAYS

BACK IN MY CATERING days, I made special bites for the kids at the event. I noticed that any time I included deviled eggs, the adults would wipe the kids' plates clean of them, so I came up with these versions for a more grown-up palate. What I love about deviled eggs is that no matter how you dress them up, they're still informal and fun. You can easily scale up any of the filling recipes if you want to stick with one or two varieties.

MAKES 12 HALVES (4 OF EACH KIND) · ACTIVE: 30 MIN · TOTAL: 45 MIN

6 large eggs

Fine sea salt and freshly ground black pepper

Place the eggs in a saucepan, cover them with cold water by 1 inch, and bring to a boil over medium heat. As soon as the water boils, immediately turn off the heat and let sit for 15 minutes. Transfer the eggs with a slotted spoon to a bowl of ice water and submerge them for 10 minutes to stop cooking. Peel, cut in half lengthwise, and separate the yolks from the whites.

Season the empty egg whites with a light dusting of salt and black pepper.

SMOKY CRAB

2 ounces lump crabmeat, picked free of shells and well drained

2 hard-boiled egg yolks, crumbled

1 tablespoon finely chopped celery

2 tablespoons mayonnaise

½ teaspoon smoked paprika

¼ teaspoon Old Bay seasoning

Dash of Tabasco sauce

Dill sprigs, for garnish

In a small bowl, mash together the crabmeat, egg yolks, celery, mayonnaise, paprika, Old Bay, and Tabasco. Use a spoon to fill 4 of the egg whites, and top each one with a sprig of dill.

{ RECIPE CONTINUES }

LOVAGE AND BACON

2 hard-boiled egg yolks, crumbled

2 tablespoons finely chopped celery

1 tablespoon crumbled cooked bacon or pancetta

1 tablespoon mayonnaise

1 teaspoon thinly sliced fresh lovage or celery leaves

Pinch of fine sea salt

In a small bowl, mash everything together with a large fork. Use a spoon to fill 4 of the egg whites.

CAESAR

2 hard-boiled egg yolks, crumbled

2 tablespoons finely grated Parmigiano-Reggiano

1 tablespoon mayonnaise

1 teaspoon finely chopped oil-packed anchovies

1 teaspoon finely grated lemon zest

1 teaspoon sliced fresh chives or scallions or Roasted Garlic Puree (page 77)

Dash of Worcestershire sauce

Freshly ground black pepper

Fine sea salt (optional)

4 to 8 small arugula leaves

In a small bowl, mash the egg yolks, cheese, mayonnaise, anchovies, lemon zest, chives, Worcestershire, and one turn of black pepper using a large fork. Taste and season with salt if needed. Use a spoon to fill 4 of the egg whites, and top each one with 1 or 2 arugula leaves.

BAKED FARMER'S EGGS

AMONG BREAKFAST'S GREATEST HITS is the homey, hearty egg casserole. If you don't have one in your repertoire yet, this is one to get to know by heart. It's ideal for prepping the day before and baking the next morning. Think of it like a frittata—you can throw just about anything into the mix, from leftover roasted vegetables to whatever herbs and cheese you have in your fridge. You can also serve it at room temperature or reheat it, covered, in a low oven.

SERVES 4 TO 6 · ACTIVE: 20 MIN · TOTAL: 1 HR

Unsalted butter, for greasing the pan

8 large eggs

1 cup heavy cream

½ cup milk

1 cup finely grated Parmigiano-Reggiano

Fine sea salt

8 ounces thick-sliced bacon, cut into ¼-inch pieces

1 pound fingerling potatoes, diced (about 1 cup)

2 scallions, cut into ¼-inch pieces

1 tablespoon sliced fresh flat-leaf parsley

1 tablespoon chopped fresh dill

½ large baguette or rustic bread torn into bite-size pieces (about 5 cups)

2 cups grated cheddar cheese

Freshly ground black pepper

Preheat the oven to 325°F. Generously butter a 9 x 13-inch baking dish.

Whisk together the eggs, cream, milk, Parmigiano, and a couple of pinches of salt until completely combined.

Place the bacon and potatoes in a large skillet and add just enough water to cover. Cook over medium heat until the water evaporates and the bacon starts to brown and the potatoes are tender, about 10 minutes. Remove from the heat and stir in the scallions, parsley, and dill.

Scatter the torn bread evenly in the buttered baking dish. Sprinkle the bacon and potato mixture and 1 cup of the cheddar cheese evenly over the bread. Slowly pour in the egg mixture. Bake for 25 minutes. Sprinkle the remaining 1 cup cheddar cheese on top of the eggs and bake until the cheese is melted and starting to brown and the center is hot, about 15 minutes longer. Remove from the oven, top with two turns of black pepper, and let sit for 5 minutes to firm up.

TANDOORI CHICKEN

MARINATING CHICKEN IN YOGURT and spices adds moisture and exotic flavor, so it's always been a favorite of mine at Indian restaurants. Serve it hot or cold with a side of basmati rice; a cool, crisp salad; or Sautéed Cucumbers with Spearmint, Cilantro, and Lime (page 39). It's also a solid choice for a picnic or travel day, either on its own or sliced for sandwiches.

SERVES 4 · ACTIVE: 20 MIN · TOTAL: I HR IO MIN, PLUS 4 HR TO 2 DAYS FOR MARINATING

2 tablespoons cumin seeds

2 tablespoons sweet paprika

2 tablespoons smoked paprika

1 tablespoon coriander seeds

1 tablespoon fennel seeds

1 teaspoon whole black peppercorns

1 teaspoon fine sea salt

¼ teaspoon red pepper flakes

2 garlic cloves, peeled

2 tablespoons peeled and finely chopped fresh ginger

Finely grated zest and juice of 1 large lemon

Finely grated zest and juice of 1 lime

2 cups whole-milk yogurt

1 (3½- to 5-pound) chicken, cut into 8 pieces (drumsticks, thighs, breasts, wings)

Blend the cumin seeds, sweet and smoked paprikas, coriander seeds, fennel seeds, peppercorns, salt, and red pepper flakes in a blender until they become a fine powder.

Add the garlic cloves, ginger, and lemon and lime zests and juice, and blend until smooth. Scrape down the sides with a rubber spatula. Add the yogurt and pulse on and off until all the ingredients are combined.

In a glass bowl or baking dish, thoroughly coat the chicken pieces with half the yogurt marinade (refrigerate or freeze the rest for up to one month for another recipe). Cover and marinate in the refrigerator for at least 4 hours and up to 2 days.

Preheat the oven to 325°F. Line a baking sheet with aluminum foil and arrange a roasting rack on top.

Remove the chicken from the marinade, leaving a generous coating on each piece. Place the chicken skin side up on the roasting rack. Leave at least ½ inch between pieces. Spoon any extra marinade from the bowl on top of the pieces.

Roast the chicken until it reaches an internal temperature of 160°F, about 45 minutes. Turn the oven broiler on low and broil the chicken until the yogurt marinade starts to slightly blacken, about 5 minutes. If your oven doesn't have a broiler, crank the oven to 450°F and brown the chicken for about 5 minutes.

TURMERIC CHICKEN

with Artichokes and Basil Yogurt

WHEN I COOK CHICKEN, I usually prefer the juicy, slightly rich dark meat from the thighs, but this marinade is an excellent way to give life to unexciting chicken breasts. Yogurt adds a nice tart richness to this dish and helps tenderize the meat.

SERVES 4 TO 6 · ACTIVE: 45 MIN ·
TOTAL: 1 HR 45 MIN, PLUS 2 HR TO 1 DAY FOR MARINATING

¼ cup plain Greek yogurt

1½ teaspoons Old Bay seasoning

2 teaspoons ground turmeric

1 pound boneless, skinless chicken thighs and/or breasts, cut into 1-inch pieces

¼ cup rice flour

¼ cup all-purpose flour

Freshly ground black pepper

¼ cup extra-virgin olive oil

12 baby artichokes, outer leaves removed, stem peeled, and halved

Fine sea salt

Finely grated zest of 1 lime

2 tablespoons sliced fresh flat-leaf parsley

2 tablespoons finely sliced fresh chives

Basil Yogurt, for serving (recipe follows)

In a medium bowl, whisk together the yogurt, Old Bay, and 1 teaspoon of the turmeric. Add the chicken and toss to coat. Cover and marinate in the refrigerator for at least 2 hours and up to 1 day.

Preheat the oven to 375°F.

Sift together both flours, the remaining 1 teaspoon turmeric, and 10 turns of coarsely cracked black pepper in a shallow dish. Place the marinated chicken in a strainer and shake off any excess marinade. Dust each piece of chicken in the flour mixture, entirely coating the pieces.

Pour 2 tablespoons of the olive oil into a skillet or roasting pan and put it in the preheated oven along with another dry skillet or pan. Heat both pans for 5 minutes.

Toss the artichokes in a bowl with the remaining 2 tablespoons olive oil and ¼ teaspoon salt. Add them to the preheated, unoiled skillet, cut side down in one layer. Roast until they're tender and the bottoms are golden brown, 15 to 20 minutes. At the same time, add the chicken to the preheated, oiled pan and roast for about 8 minutes on each side.

In a serving dish, toss together the chicken, artichokes, lime zest, parsley, and chives. Drizzle with basil yogurt and serve.

BASIL YOGURT

MAKES ABOUT 1 CUP

This can be made a day ahead and kept in the fridge until you're ready to drizzle it over the chicken. It's great on grilled fish, sliced beefsteak or heirloom tomatoes, or just about anything spicy.

Fine sea salt

1 cup fresh basil leaves

¾ cup plain Greek yogurt

1 small shallot, thinly sliced

Juice of 1 lime

1 tablespoon light-flavored honey

1 tablespoon extra-virgin olive oil

Bring a small saucepan of salted water to a boil. Blanch the basil leaves in the boiling water for 10 minutes. Rinse in cold water for a few seconds to cool, then drain, dry, and coarsely chop them.

Combine the basil, yogurt, shallot, lime juice, honey, olive oil, and ¼ teaspoon salt in a blender and blend until pureed, about 2 minutes. Add a little cold water to get things moving, if necessary. Refrigerate in an airtight container for up to 24 hours.

SAVORY-STUFFED SKILLET CHICKEN
with Lemon-Miso Sauce

THIS TRADITIONAL STUFFING SANDWICHED between juicy meat and crispy skin starts to transport you to Thanksgiving, but a creamy, tangy lemon-miso sauce replaces ordinary gravy to cut the richness of the stuffing and make an otherwise ordinary dish exceptional.

SERVES 4 · ACTIVE: 25 MIN · TOTAL: I HR IO MIN

1 (3½-pound) chicken

2 cups cubed bread, preferably brioche

2 tablespoons chopped fresh savory

1 tablespoon sliced fresh flat-leaf parsley

1 teaspoon Old Bay seasoning

1 teaspoon finely grated lemon zest

2 tablespoons Roasted Garlic Puree (page 77) or 1 tablespoon minced garlic

6 tablespoons unsalted butter; 4 tablespoons cubed and 2 tablespoons melted

Fine sea salt and freshly ground black pepper

½ cup Lemon-Miso Sauce (page 210)

Position a rack in the bottom of the oven and preheat the oven to 350°F.

Remove the neck and giblets from the chicken. Place the chicken on a cutting board, breast side down. Working from the cavity opening up to the neck, cut along each side of the backbone with a pair of kitchen shears. Discard the backbone. Cut down the middle of the chicken through the breastbone to cut it in half.

In a food processor with the blade attachment, buzz the bread, savory, parsley, Old Bay, and lemon zest until the bread turns to crumbs. Add the garlic and cubed butter and spin until just combined and the mixture has a crumbly texture.

Starting at the top center of the breast, gently separate the skin from the meat until a pocket forms from the top of the breast to the drumstick. Place half the stuffing under the skin of each chicken half, spreading it in a smooth, even layer. Brush the skin generously with the melted butter and lightly season all over with salt and pepper. Place skin side down in a large cast-iron or enameled cast-iron baking pan. Roast on the bottom rack until the skin is golden brown and crispy and the chicken reaches an internal temperature of 165°F, about 45 minutes. Remove from the oven, turn the chicken over, and let it rest skin side up in the pan for a few minutes. Serve with the lemon-miso sauce on the side.

LEMON-MISO SAUCE

MAKES ABOUT ½ CUP · ACTIVE: 15 MIN · TOTAL: 30 MIN

This easy pan sauce can be made in the skillet while the chicken rests, or separately while the chicken cooks. It also pairs well with pork or duck.

1 garlic clove, peeled

1 small shallot, peeled

1 celery stalk

1 small carrot

1 tablespoon unsalted butter

1 cup dry white wine

2 tablespoons white miso

2 cups Chicken Stock (page 293)

1 tablespoon freshly squeezed
   lemon juice

1 tablespoon sliced fresh flat-leaf parsley

Small pinch of red pepper flakes

Finely chop the garlic, shallot, celery, and carrot in a food processor. Melt the butter in a medium saucepan over medium-low heat and sweat the vegetables in the butter until they just start to brown, about 5 minutes. Add the wine and reduce until almost dry, about 5 minutes. Stir in the miso and then pour in the chicken stock. Simmer until the sauce is thick enough to coat the back of a spoon, about 15 minutes. Add the lemon juice, parsley, and red pepper flakes. Taste and adjust the seasoning as needed.

A Learned Skill

"I'm a horrible cook." It's a comment I hear frequently when I tell people I'm a chef. I used to just shrug my shoulders and feel sorry for them for having to eat all that bad food. But then I got curious and started asking questions: "Do you cook a lot?" "Have you ever taken a class or had anyone teach you?"

It's okay if eating is more your thing than cooking. But if you're passionate about cooking and just don't feel successful, get some help. Cooking is a learned skill. Some people are truly gifted and make heavenly food from the start, but most cooks learn the craft. Watching cooking shows on TV doesn't really do it. Yes, they can be informative, educational, and entertaining—but they're mostly just entertaining. Watching a cooking show and trying to learn how to cook is like listening to Yo-Yo Ma play Bach or Jimi Hendrix make love to his Stratocaster and believing you can replicate those emotionally stirring sounds at will.

One of the best ways to learn to cook is by helping out good cooks (such as friends or relatives) when they host a dinner party, or volunteering your time to work with a community kitchen. It's a win-win deal: They get an extra set of hands and you get to learn some new skills. Take a class, help a friend, and learn to be a better cook. It doesn't always come naturally. ❧

GLAZED BRAISED PORK BELLY

with Beans and Fennel

AS A KID, MY favorite dinner on family camping trips was baked beans and hot dogs. Fat, salt, and sugar—what's not to like? Years later, I wanted a grown-up version, and came up with this dish. A note on fennel pollen: A little of it goes a long way, and while it doesn't come cheap, it adds an anise flavor that can't be replicated and brings out the perfume of high-quality pork.

SERVES 4 · ACTIVE: 30 MIN · TOTAL: 3 HR, PLUS OVERNIGHT FOR SOAKING

1 cup dried cannellini beans

2 small carrots, cut into 1 inch pieces

1 fennel bulb, core removed and cut into ½-inch slices

1 small white onion, cut into ½-inch slices

1 celery stalk, cut into 1-inch pieces

3 garlic cloves; 2 cloves smashed and 1 minced

1 bay leaf

2 rosemary sprigs

1 cup freshly squeezed orange juice

Fine sea salt and black pepper

1½ pounds boneless, skinless pork belly

1 shallot, thinly sliced

¼ cup buckwheat honey

¼ cup sherry vinegar

Pinch of red pepper flakes

Pinch of fennel pollen (optional)

2 tablespoons chopped fennel fronds

2 tablespoons sliced fresh flat-leaf parsley

Soak the beans overnight in a large bowl covered with plenty of cold water.

Position a rack in the center of the oven and preheat the oven to 325°F.

Put the (drained) beans, carrots, fennel, onion, celery, smashed garlic, bay leaf, rosemary, orange juice, and a pinch of salt in a large Dutch oven. Lightly season the pork with salt and pepper on both sides and place on top of the vegetables. Add enough cold water to just cover the pork. Transfer the pot to the oven and cook until the belly is very tender when poked with a fork, 2 hours to 2 hours and 30 minutes.

Remove the belly from the Dutch oven and cut into 4 large pieces. Heat a large sauté pan over medium heat and, starting with the skin side down first, brown each side of the pork pieces for about 5 minutes. Transfer the pork to a paper towel–lined plate. Pour out all but about 1 tablespoon of fat from the pan. Add the shallot and cook until it begins to brown. Add the minced garlic and the honey. Cook until the honey starts to bubble, about 1 minute, then add the vinegar (you might want to turn on the stove vent!) and reduce by half.

Ladle out 2 cups of cooking liquid from the Dutch oven and add it to the pan, along with the red pepper flakes. Reduce for about 10 minutes, until the liquid reaches the consistency of maple syrup. Add the pork belly pieces back to the pan and baste for a few minutes, until they're coated and take on a golden, lacquered appearance. Sprinkle in the fennel pollen and baste a few more times.

Remove the bay leaf and rosemary stems from the bean and vegetable mixture. Mix in the fennel fronds and parsley. Taste and adjust the seasoning as needed, and then place the glazed belly on top. Drizzle any extra glaze on top, add a few turns of black pepper, and serve.

BLACKBERRY-BASTED PORK TENDERLOIN

TENDERLOIN IS AN EASY cut to work with—it's boneless, very tender, and takes well to searing, roasting, and grilling. It's usually on the lean side, so the key is to not overcook it. The savory-sweet marinade here will help you out with that, keeping the pork moist while it roasts. Serve this with a hearty salad like Black Kale and Cabbage Salad (page 60), and save any leftovers for an amazing sandwich the next day.

SERVES 4 · ACTIVE: 20 MIN ·
TOTAL: I HR 20 MIN, PLUS 2 HR TO I DAY FOR MARINATING

1 pint fresh blackberries (or other fresh berries; frozen will work too)

2 tablespoons soy sauce or tamari

2 tablespoons mirin or light honey

1 teaspoon Chinese five-spice powder

2 pork tenderloins (about 2 pounds total), preferably a heritage breed, cleaned, silverskin removed

Coarse sea salt and freshly ground black pepper

In a blender, puree the blackberries, soy sauce, mirin, and Chinese five-spice. Divide the sauce in half; pour one half into a shallow baking dish and reserve the other half in the refrigerator. Pat the pork dry and marinate in the baking dish for at least 2 hours and up to 1 day, covering it in the marinade and flipping the tenderloin once halfway through.

Preheat the oven to 375°F. Cover a baking sheet with aluminum foil and arrange a roasting rack on top.

Remove the pork from the blackberry marinade and place the pork on the roasting rack. Roast for 20 minutes, brushing the tenderloin with the reserved blackberry mixture after 10 minutes. Turn the pork over and continue roasting and basting with the sauce every 10 minutes for another 20 minutes, or until the internal temperature reaches 155°F in the thickest part of the meat. Let the pork rest in a warm place for 5 minutes. Thinly slice the pork and season with coarse salt and black pepper.

CIDER-GLAZED PORK CHOPS
with Sage and Apples

THIS DISH IS ON heavy rotation at my place when fall comes around. I love the aroma of hot apple cider and sage wafting though the kitchen as the sauce reduces. There's a strong comfort-food vibe to moist, juicy pork chops fully coated in a cider glaze, especially when they're served with apples and sage. I always go for heritage-breed pork like Hampshire or Berkshire; they're juicier and have an infinitely more complex flavor. If you like heat, add a pinch of red pepper flakes to the glaze when you stir in the cider vinegar.

SERVES 4 · ACTIVE: 25 MINUTES · TOTAL: 25 MIN

4 (10- to 12-ounce) bone-in pork chops, about 1 inch thick

Fine sea salt and freshly ground black pepper

2 tablespoons extra-virgin olive oil

1 tablespoon unsalted butter

1 shallot, thinly sliced

2 apples, peeled, cored, and diced

1 garlic clove, finely chopped

1 tablespoon apple cider vinegar

2 cups fresh apple cider

2 tablespoons chopped fresh sage

1 tablespoon sliced fresh chives

Preheat the oven to 350°F. Line a baking sheet with aluminum foil and arrange a roasting rack on top.

Pat the pork chops dry with paper towels. Season them all over with salt and pepper.

In a large skillet, heat the olive oil over high heat. Add the pork chops to the pan, leaving 2 inches between them. (Cook in batches, if necessary.) Sear on both sides until golden brown, 2 to 3 minutes per side.

Transfer the pork chops to the roasting rack and roast until the internal temperature of the chops reaches 155°F next to the bone, about 10 minutes. Let the pork chops rest for 5 minutes.

Make the cider glaze in the same skillet used to sear the chops. Wipe out any excess oil. Melt the butter in the skillet over medium-low heat. Add the shallot and apples and cook until the shallots are translucent and tender, about 3 minutes. Stir in the garlic and cook for another minute without browning, until you get a whiff of its aroma. Add the vinegar

and reduce until almost dry, about 1 minute. Add the apple cider, sage, and ¼ teaspoon salt. Cook until the glaze is shiny and thick enough to coat the pork chops, about 10 minutes.

Put the pork chops on a plate or serving platter and pour the apples and glaze over them. Sprinkle with the chives and serve.

PORK LOIN

Crusted with Pecans and Mustard

THIS RECIPE FIRST CAME together at the last minute at my sister's house, as I foraged in her pantry for ingredients while cooking for an unexpected dinner party. The guests were impressed, and it has become one of her go-to dishes for simplicity and convenience. I originally used chicken, but the pronounced flavor of pork works even better with the mustard and pecans. Coating the loin in mustard adds moisture to the lean cut, and salty crushed pecans give it a little elegance. Serve the pork alongside Baby Bok Choy with Red Pepper Sauce (page 118) for a killer weeknight dinner. Don't worry if some of the crust comes off in the oven. Just spoon it over the finished dish—it's just as delicious.

SERVES 4 · ACTIVE: 10 MIN · TOTAL: 30 MIN

2 large egg whites

¼ cup smooth Dijon mustard

1 teaspoon finely chopped fresh chives

2 cups finely crushed pecans

¼ teaspoon fine sea salt

4 (6-ounce) pieces pork loin, trimmed and pounded to a ½-inch thickness

1 tablespoon avocado oil

Preheat the oven to 350°F.

In a large bowl, whisk together the egg whites, mustard, and chives. Mix the pecans and the salt together in a shallow pan or plate.

Pat the pork dry with a paper towel and dip it into the mustard mixture, thoroughly coating each piece. Shake off the excess mustard, but leave a fairly heavy coating. Firmly press each piece of pork into the pecans, coating evenly on both sides.

Pour the oil into a large skillet (or line a baking sheet with aluminum foil and coat the foil with the oil) and place the pork in the skillet (or baking sheet). Roast until the pecans start to brown and the pork feels firm to the touch and a meat thermometer reads 145°F, 15 to 20 minutes. Serve immediately.

Aroma and Acid

I like to marinate all the meat, poultry, and fish I cook with. It adds complexity and depth of flavor to your cooking, and it helps prevent raw fish and meats from taking on refrigerator scents. There are two kinds of marinade: aromatic (non-acidic) and acidic.

Aromatic, NON-ACIDIC MARINADES don't use vinegar or wine, but add flavor with herbs, spices, aromatics, and oil. The oil keeps proteins moist but not wet, thereby extending their shelf life, and prevents oxidation by inhibiting the growth of oxygen-loving bacteria. Thyme, rosemary, and garlic all contain antibacterial compounds as well. If you're growing herbs, this is a great way to use the stems and dry leaves. I also marinate dense, fatty fish like salmon, bluefish, butterfish, swordfish, shark, and tuna—try using the tandoori sauce (page 204) on salmon or bluefish. Adding flavor can be as simple as coating a piece of meat with some crushed bay leaf, black pepper, and a little oil. Oil-based aromatic marinades will help prevent food from sticking to a pan or grill, but be sure to wipe off any excess oil before you grill so that you don't have a flare-up.

ACIDIC MARINADES use wine, vinegar, and fruit juices like citrus and pomegranate to add flavor, preserve, and tenderize. They can also "cook" foods like ceviche, which you want to avoid unless that's the desired effect, as in Scallops Marinated with Horseradish and Lemon Thyme (page 177). If marinated too long in an acidic marinade or the acidity is too high, proteins "burn." Balsamic-Soy Marinated Hanger Steak (page 220) and Tandoori Chicken (page 204) are two different examples of an acidic marinade. See pages 290–291 for basic aromatic and acidic marinades for meat and fish. ❧

BALSAMIC-SOY MARINATED
HANGER STEAK

WHY HANGER STEAK? If New York strip is Manhattan's cut, then the hanger must be Brooklyn's—dense, rich, full of character. It's also a great alternative to more expensive cuts, offering bold flavor at a reasonable price. No wonder it's a mainstay on Brooklyn restaurant menus.

This cut is best cooked quickly on high heat and served rare to medium-rare—past that and it gets tough. You have to plan ahead since the steak requires at least a night to bathe in the marinade, but it's well worth it. The acidity and salt in the marinade tenderize the meat for a nicely charred exterior. You can marinate the pieces for up to 2 days—the longer, the better. Just keep turning them occasionally. Serve the steak with Cipollini Onion Brûlée with Balsamic Vinegar and Rosemary (page 72) and a good potato salad.

SERVES 4 · ACTIVE: 15 MIN · TOTAL: 25 MIN, PLUS OVERNIGHT FOR MARINATING

¼ cup balsamic vinegar

¼ cup soy sauce

1 tablespoon vegetable oil, plus more
 for grilling

½ teaspoon freshly ground black pepper

4 garlic cloves, smashed

1 thyme sprig

2 pounds hanger steak, fat trimmed, cut
 crosswise into 4 pieces (top sirloin tips
 cut across the grain into 2-inch strips
 also work well)

In a glass or nonreactive baking dish, whisk together the balsamic vinegar, soy sauce, vegetable oil, and pepper. Add the garlic and thyme sprig. Put the steaks in the dish and baste them with the marinade until coated. Cover the dish with plastic wrap and refrigerate overnight (at least 12 hours), turning the steaks over at least once.

Remove the steaks from the marinade and pat dry with paper towels.

Prepare a hot grill and oil the grill rack, or heat a grill pan on the stovetop over medium-high heat and brush the pan with vegetable oil. Grill the steaks until medium-rare with an internal temperature of 125°F, 4 to 6 minutes per side.

Transfer the steaks to a plate, cover loosely with aluminum foil, and let them rest for 5 minutes. Thinly slice the steaks against the grain and serve.

DRY-RUBBED PORTERHOUSE

with Tamarind Steak Sauce

MARINADES HAVE THEIR MERITS, but for grilled steaks with more powerful, deeper flavor, I go with a dry rub. Storing the dry-rubbed steaks in the refrigerator allows time for the spices to work their way into the meat and make it taste like it's been aged. You can skip this step and grill the meat right away, but you'll sacrifice some intensity in flavor. Other bone-in cuts, like rib eye or New York strip, also take well to a dry rub.

SERVES 4 · ACTIVE: 5 MIN · TOTAL: 20 MIN, PLUS 2 HR TO 1 DAY FOR THE RUB

¼ cup paprika

1 tablespoon dried thyme

1 tablespoon ground coriander

1 tablespoon fine sea salt

1 teaspoon freshly ground black pepper

1 teaspoon ground mustard

1 teaspoon dried marjoram

1 teaspoon onion powder

½ teaspoon garlic powder

4 (12-ounce) porterhouse steaks, about 1 inch thick

Tamarind Steak Sauce, for serving (page 224)

Combine the paprika, thyme, coriander, salt, pepper, ground mustard, marjoram, onion powder, and garlic powder in a bowl. Pat the steaks dry and rub a generous amount of the spice mix on all sides. Wrap them in parchment paper and store in an airtight container in the refrigerator for at least 2 hours and up to 1 day.

Prepare a hot grill and oil the grill rack. Remove the steaks from the refrigerator about 20 minutes before cooking.

Put the steaks on the hot part of the grill and sear for about 4 minutes on each side. The goal is to get a crispy char. Move the steaks to a cooler part of the grill and continue to cook until the internal temperature near the bone reaches 135°F for medium-rare, 3 to 4 minutes more. Let the steaks rest uncovered for 5 minutes in a warm place. Serve with the tamarind steak sauce on the side.

TAMARIND STEAK SAUCE

MAKES ABOUT 1 CUP · ACTIVE: 10 MIN · TOTAL: 1 HR

This is a total umami-bomb of a steak sauce: mushrooms, tamari, Parmigiano rind. Tart tamarind, used frequently in Asian and Indian cuisines, balances the deep savoriness of steak and cuts through its fat. The sauce's sweetness comes from the onions, so it's important to get them nice and caramelized.

2 tablespoons extra-virgin olive oil

1 medium yellow onion, thinly sliced

2 garlic cloves, chopped

1 cup sliced button mushrooms or mushroom scraps

1 cup red wine vinegar

1 teaspoon whole black peppercorns

¼ teaspoon ground cloves

¼ teaspoon ground allspice

¼ teaspoon ground nutmeg

½ cup tamari or soy sauce

¼ cup tamarind concentrate

1 small piece Parmigiano-Reggiano rind (optional)

Heat the olive oil in a medium pot over medium-low heat. Add the onion, garlic, and mushrooms. Cook until the onions start to brown, about 5 minutes, stirring occasionally.

Add the vinegar, peppercorns, cloves, allspice, and nutmeg, and continue cooking until the vinegar has almost completely evaporated, about 5 minutes. Add the tamari, tamarind, cheese rind (if using), and 1 cup water. Simmer gently for 20 minutes. Remove from the heat and set aside at room temperature to let the flavors blend for 30 minutes.

Pour the mixture through a fine-mesh sieve set over a bowl. Press the back of a ladle against the vegetables to release all the liquid they absorbed. The sauce can be used immediately, or store it in the refrigerator in an airtight container for up to 2 weeks.

POMEGRANATE-BRAISED LAMB SHANKS

BRAISES ARE MY FAVORITE kind of lazy weekend recipes—the kind where the oven does the work of creating delicious, tender, falling-off-the-bone meat, while an intoxicating aroma fills your kitchen. Here, I give lamb shanks, an inexpensive comfort food, a boost with sweet-tart pomegranate juice and warming whole spices.

SERVES 4 · ACTIVE: 30 MIN · TOTAL: 3 HR

1 cup all-purpose flour

1 tablespoon fine sea salt

1 tablespoon freshly ground black pepper

4 (12-ounce) lamb shanks

2 tablespoons extra-virgin olive oil

2 celery stalks, diced

1 small yellow onion, diced

1 large carrot, peeled and diced

4 garlic cloves, smashed

3 cups pomegranate juice

3 cups Chicken Stock (page 293) or water, plus more if needed

1 tablespoon coriander seeds

1 tablespoon fennel seeds

2 tablespoons sliced fresh flat-leaf parsley

¼ cup pomegranate seeds

Preheat the oven to 300°F.

Mix the flour, salt, and pepper in a large bowl. Pat the shanks dry and dredge them in the flour one by one. In a Dutch oven, heat the olive oil over medium heat. Brown the shanks for 4 to 5 minutes per side, developing a good bronze color on both sides. Remove from the pot.

In the same pot over medium heat, cook the celery, onion, and carrot until lightly browned, about 5 minutes, then add the garlic and cook for another minute. Place the shanks on top of the vegetables in the pot. Add the pomegranate juice and chicken stock, making sure the shanks are fully covered by the liquid (if necessary, add more stock to cover them). Bring to a simmer.

While the braise is coming to a simmer, place the coriander seeds and fennel seeds in a piece of cheesecloth and create a loose pouch tied with kitchen twine (a tea ball would work here too). Submerge the spice pouch in the simmering liquid. Cover with a tight-fitting lid or aluminum foil and cook until the meat is fork-tender and coming off the bone, about 1 hour and 30 minutes. Remove the lid and continue to cook for another 30 minutes, spooning the braising liquid over the meat every 10 minutes.

Remove the spice pouch. Sprinkle with the parsley and pomegranate seeds and serve.

Do Small Things Well

Even the most complex recipes are the sum of many simple acts like searing.
Putting those small acts together makes a great cook.

Searing gives complexity of flavor and adds texture by creating a crust. However, it doesn't seal in juices or keep ingredients moist, as kitchen lore suggests.

If you use a heavy pan with the right amount and type of oil and the right heat, the pan will get hot enough, retain heat well, and not smoke up the place. Making sure the food is free of moisture from water or water-based marinades is important. The moisture causes steam which slows the searing process and drops the temperature. Ingredients that are dry or very lightly and evenly coated in oil sear better.

Searing begins at around 300°F for dry ingredients. Extra-virgin olive oil has a smoke point of approximately 375°F. So, you can sear food with olive oil, but if the heat level exceeds its smoking point, you'll have a smoky kitchen and acrid-tasting food. The higher the smoke point of the oil, the lower the chances of causing havoc with fire alarms, nervous pets, a smelly house, and teary eyes. Admittedly, it's hard to control the temperature of a pan on a stovetop. A skilled cook is constantly adjusting the heat to get it just right.

At home, I like to oven-sear for more accuracy and less smoke. If your oven is set to 375°F, the pan won't get hotter than that. Also, the oven keeps a food's aroma contained to a certain extent (so your whole house doesn't smell like fish for days after cooking it). To properly sear in the oven, I wait until the oven is fully preheated, then I heat the pan I'll be cooking with. I use a heavy cast-iron flat skillet or an enamel-coated cast-iron double-burner skinny skillet. A grill pan works well too, if you're after the look of grill marks.

Tossing your ingredients in a bowl with a small amount of oil and seasoning ensures that everything is evenly coated and that you're not using too much oil. The food should sizzle a little when it hits the preheated pan. Of course, be careful pulling the preheated pan out of the oven to add the ingredients, as it will be very hot. For even searing, stir cut foods every 5 to 10 minutes and occasionally flip large portions.

Whether cooking on the stovetop or in the oven, avoid searing with too much cooking oil. It can splatter and make a mess of your oven, not to mention smoke a lot. There's also the slim chance of hot oil splattering and hitting the heating element or flame and igniting. If the food is free of excess moisture and the temperature is right, this won't happen.

I cringe when I see cooks unwrap fish or meat from plastic-wrapped packages and put it directly into a hot pan. The moisture on food that has lived in a plastic package for days creates steam when cooked, which interferes with browning and toughens up the protein, compromising taste. That's why fishmongers and butchers wrap food in waxed or butcher

paper. Unlike plastic, these wrappers keep meat and fish free from excess moisture. Dry meat sears better, absorbs flavor more efficiently, and tastes fresher.

When I get back from the market, I remove ingredients from their packaging and store them in a way that helps them retain their freshness. Dry off meat and fish with a paper towel and wrap them in butcher or parchment paper, then place them in a glass dish sealed with a lid. If freezing food, dry it, marinate it in an aromatic marinade, and freeze in an airtight glass container labeled with the date and contents. The freezing and storing process enhances the effect of the marinade, and in turn, the marinade coats the food, preventing freezer burn and that weird freezer taste.

Here's another key to proper searing, which is true for blanching as well: Don't overcrowd the pan or pot. Placing too much food in at one time causes a quick drop in temperature. Instead of the high-heat, rapid cooking you want for searing, the food in the pan will steam. When blanched in an overcrowded pot of boiling water, green vegetables lose their color and vibrancy. Cook in batches, if necessary. If you're cooking a big meal, you might need to strategize oven and stovetop space. It might take more time, but it will be worth it in terms of the flavor, color, and texture of your dish. ❧

LAMB SIRLOIN
Crusted with Cocoa and Cumin

WHEN I COOK LAMB, I typically choose something other than the ubiquitous rack of lamb. Animals have lots of parts and they all need to be used—so use them! Lamb sirloin is a dense, inexpensive cut that's tender enough for roasting or grilling. It's not as easy to find as the ever-popular rib rack or leg of lamb, but a local butcher should have it. The cocoa-cumin rub is subtler than you might think and gives the lamb a deeper, earthy flavor and intense dark color—so dark it may appear burnt before slicing and revealing the juicy red meat inside, though it's not. For best results, marinate the lamb overnight in the Basic Aromatic Marinade for Meat (page 290) before cooking. Serve it with roasted root vegetables or with Bitter Greens with Dates, Sesame, and Warm Goat Cheese (page 30).

SERVES 4 · ACTIVE: 10 MIN · TOTAL: 25 MIN

4 (6- to 8-ounce) pieces boneless lamb sirloin or lamb loin

¼ cup unsweetened raw cacao powder

2 tablespoons ground cumin

¼ teaspoon fine sea salt

Freshly ground black pepper

1 tablespoon avocado or olive oil

Preheat the oven to 350°F.

Pat the lamb dry and remove any excess fat or sinew. In a bowl, mix together the cacao powder, cumin, salt, and two turns of black pepper. Dredge the lamb in the seasoning until lightly coated on all sides.

Heat the avocado oil in a large pan over medium-high heat. Add the lamb and sear on both sides until dark brown, 1 to 2 minutes per side.

Transfer the pan to the oven and roast for 10 to 15 minutes (if using lamb loin, it'll be a few minutes less); start checking for doneness after about 8 minutes. The internal temperature should reach 130°F for medium-rare. Remove the lamb from the oven and let rest in a warm place for about 5 minutes. Thinly slice against the grain and serve.

LAMB AND GOAT CHEESE PASTIES

EVERY ETHNIC DELI IN Brooklyn has some version of this traditional "grab and go" fast food. This pasty with lamb and goat cheese is cozy, rich, uncomplicated, and exactly what I want to eat after a day outside frolicking in (or trudging through) the snow.

MAKES 12 PASTIES · ACTIVE: 30 MIN · TOTAL: 1 HR

1 tablespoon extra-virgin olive oil

8 ounces ground lamb

6 scallions or ramps, thinly sliced

2 plum tomatoes, diced

½ cup goat cheese

¼ cup loosely packed fresh flat-leaf parsley, chopped

2 tablespoons Kalamata olives, pitted and finely chopped

Fine sea salt and freshly ground black pepper

¼ cup all-purpose flour

1 Savory Tart Crust (page 284)

1 large egg yolk

Sweet Marjoram Chimichurri (page 20), for serving

In a large skillet, heat the olive oil over medium heat. Add the lamb and cook until browned, stirring occasionally to break it up, about 5 minutes. Transfer to a bowl and let the lamb cool. Add the scallions, tomatoes, cheese, parsley, and olives to the bowl. Season with salt and black pepper and put the bowl in the fridge to chill while you prep the dough.

Position a rack in the center of the oven and preheat the oven to 350°F. Line a baking sheet with parchment paper.

Sprinkle the flour on a clean work surface and shape the tart dough into logs about 2 inches in diameter and 6 inches long. Cut the logs into twelve ½-inch-thick disks. Roll each disk into a ¼-inch-thick circle about 4 inches in diameter using a rolling pin—or go rustic and use an empty bottle of Bordeaux.

Whisk the egg yolk in a small bowl. Spoon about 1 tablespoon of the filling onto the bottom half of each dough circle. Brush the bottom edge with the egg wash and fold the top half over to form a half circle. Crimp the edges together with the tip of a dinner fork.

Place the pasties on the baking sheet and brush the remaining egg wash evenly over the top of them. Bake on the center rack until golden brown, about 25 minutes. Let cool for a few minutes, and serve hot or at room temperature with chimichurri on the side.

PART FOUR

COCKTAILS

The Brooklyn cocktail scene has been at the forefront of the modern mixology movement. It's a clear example of the borough's reputation for elevating a handcrafted art to new heights by mixing fresh ideas, locally sourced ingredients, and time-tested classics. Justin Lane Briggs has been my go-to cocktail guru for creating satiating and inventive cocktails. A transplant from rural Vermont, his talent embodies the best qualities of the Brooklyn Rustic style. Combining old and new, common and exotic, urban and rustic, he has created these recipes for the home bartender.

WINDOW BOX COLLINS

A TRADITIONAL TOM COLLINS is given a new life by the addition of fresh parsley syrup. The herbal flavor of the syrup complements the aromatic notes in my favorite Brooklyn-made juniper-based gin.

SERVES I

Ice cubes

2 to 3 ounces soda water, chilled, plus more if needed

2 ounces gin, preferably Greenhook Ginsmiths American Dry Gin

¾ ounce Parsley Syrup (recipe follows)

¾ ounce freshly squeezed lemon juice

1 lemon wheel, about ¼-inch thick, for garnish

1 flat-leaf parsley sprig

Fill a 12-ounce Collins glass with ice cubes and add 2 ounces soda water. In a cocktail shaker, combine the gin, parsley syrup, and lemon juice. Add ice and shake vigorously. Strain into the Collins glass and add extra soda water if needed.

Cut a small slit into the lemon wheel's edge, or bend the end of the wheel gently, to perch it on the rim of the glass. Slip the sprig of parsley and a straw alongside it.

PARSLEY SYRUP

MAKES I CUP

Making an aromatic herb syrup is an easy way to add an interesting element to classic cocktail recipes. This can be made with a variety of leafy herbs, giving you an arsenal of new flavors to play with in cocktails, iced tea, ice cream, and drizzled over fresh summer fruit.

1 cup simple syrup, chilled

½ cup loosely packed fresh flat-leaf parsley leaves or other leafy herbs

Combine the simple syrup and parsley in a blender and process on high until pureed, about 1 minute. Strain the liquid through a fine-mesh sieve. Store the syrup in a sealed glass jar in the refrigerator for up to 6 days.

Learn Your Palate

The number of tastes is infinite, since every soluble body has a special flavor
which does not wholly resemble any other.

JEAN ANTHELME BRILLAT-SAVARIN

Tasting, like cooking, is a learned skill. Learning exactly what you like is a step toward being able to re-create it. Our palates can taste sweet, sour (acidity), bitter, and salty. Umami is the fifth taste; it describes a pleasant savoriness associated with fermented foods, cured and aged meats, mushrooms, cheeses, and green tea. We each have distinct palates and preferences. Like our personalities, these are influenced by genetics, personal experiences, and cultural backgrounds.

These experiments will refine your tasting skills and strengthen the connection between your tongue and your brain. Both exercises help you identify flavors without relying on visual clues, and create an awareness of subtlety you might otherwise miss.

TASTE THRESHOLD

Try this one with a group of friends; it's an entertaining way to see how sensitive your taste buds are. Give each taster 10 cups of filtered water, numbering each cup from 1 to 10. Leave the first few cups plain. Keeping track of the amount in each glass, place a drop of lemon juice or distilled white vinegar in the third or fourth glass. Place two drops in the next, and continue increasing the amount by increments of two drops until the last cup. Have the tasters silently record which cups have no acid and which ones do. This will show the tasters' sensitivity to acidic flavors. Then place the glasses out of order and have them guess which is the most acidic and which is the least acidic.

Try the same experiment with sweetness by adding simple syrup; with salinity by adding salt; and with bitterness by adding Angostura bitters.

SMELL ASSOCIATION

Gather a variety of spices, herbs, and any fresh ingredients you want. Blindfold the tasters, then have them give each ingredient a sniff and guess what it is. You'll be surprised how hard this is, even with common ingredients.

It can be a challenge to categorize and communicate sensory experiences. We've all read wine labels with distinct descriptions of the flavor and bouquet. Most of us wouldn't be able to describe those tastes that way, even though we recognize them. Taste descriptions have their own vocabulary. ❖

THE GREEN MONK

THIS DELICIOUSLY SIMPLE RIFF on a vodka gimlet highlights the brightness of mint with the addition of some sweet herbal notes from green Chartreuse, the French liqueur made by Carthusian monks.

SERVES 1

1 long mint sprig

½ ounce simple syrup, chilled

1½ ounces vodka

¾ ounce freshly squeezed lime juice

½ ounce green Chartreuse

Ice cubes

1 lime wheel, about ¼-inch thick,
    for garnish

Pull the lower mint leaves from the stem, leaving the final sprig at the top attached to the stem for garnish. Store it upside down in a glass of cool water while you make the cocktail.

In a large cocktail shaker, combine the simple syrup and mint leaves. Lightly muddle without pulverizing the mint. Add the vodka, lime juice, Chartreuse, and ice cubes and give it a good shake. Strain over fresh ice, or one large cube, into a large rocks glass.

Use a knife to punch a small hole through the center of the lime wheel. Plunge the stem of mint blooms through until it bunches up like a bouquet. Float it on the top of the cocktail, add a straw, and serve.

PARKS AND RECREATION

CUCUMBER IS AN INCREDIBLY versatile and refreshing cocktail component, and nothing pairs with it quite as well as mint. The cooling flavors make this one a go-to for hot summer days.

SERVES 1

1 long mint sprig

4 or 5 fresh mint leaves

½ ounce simple syrup

½ large cucumber, sliced into ½-inch-thick wheels

2 ounces vodka

¾ ounce freshly squeezed lime juice

½ ounce light amaro, preferably Vecchio Amaro del Capo, Cynar, or CioCiaro

Ice cubes

Pull the lower mint leaves from the stem, leaving the final sprig at the top attached for garnish. Store it upside down in a glass of cool water while you make the cocktail.

In a cocktail shaker, combine the mint leaves, simple syrup, and 2 or 3 cucumber wheels, reserving another cucumber wheel for garnish. Lightly muddle the cucumber and mint leaves, releasing the flavors without overly bruising the mint. Add the vodka, lime juice, amaro, and ice cubes and shake it up. Strain over ice or one large cube into a rocks glass.

To garnish, plunge the stem of the mint bloom through the center of the reserved cucumber wheel until it bunches up like a bouquet. Float it on the top of the cocktail, add a straw, and serve.

SMITH STREET SOUR

WITH BALSAMIC VINEGAR AND tomatoes, this recipe takes flavor cues from one of my favorite Italian neighborhoods in Brooklyn, Carroll Gardens, and puts them into a modern cocktail. To change up the flavor, add a bit of cilantro, basil, chile pepper, or thyme. In the heat of summer, replace the tomatoes with ripe strawberries, and add ½ ounce of Campari for a slightly bitter bite on the finish.

SERVES 1

2 lime wheels, about ¼-inch thick

Salt

¼ ounce Balsamic Reduction (page 287)

6 ripe cherry tomatoes

1½ ounces blanco tequila

½ ounce curaçao or triple sec, preferably Giffard or Cointreau

½ ounce freshly squeezed lime juice

Ice cubes

Rub a wheel of lime around half the circumference of the rim of a rocks glass. Cover a plate with salt and gently press the rim of the glass into the salt, creating a salted rim on half the glass.

In a cocktail shaker, combine the balsamic reduction and 3 of the cherry tomatoes and lightly muddle them together. Add the tequila, curaçao, lime juice, and ice cubes and shake. Toss a few ice cubes into the salt-rimmed glass and strain the cocktail over the ice.

To garnish, skewer the remaining 3 cherry tomatoes on a cocktail pick. Add a straw and serve.

QANDISA COCKTAIL

REMINISCENT OF A TRADITIONAL Moroccan salad, this cocktail has a sweet and savory combo of sweet carrot, bright orange, soft raisins, mint, and spice. If you can't find kümmel, a European caraway liqueur, substitute with aquavit and a teaspoon of simple syrup.

SERVES I

1½ ounces Cognac, preferably one aged less than 10 years

½ ounce fresh carrot juice

½ ounce freshly squeezed orange juice

¼ ounce kümmel, preferably Combier

1 dash aromatic bitters, preferably Angostura or Cecil & Merl

4 or 5 fresh mint leaves

Ice cubes

1 whole nutmeg or small pinch of ground nutmeg

In a cocktail shaker, combine the Cognac, carrot juice, orange juice, kümmel, bitters, and mint leaves. Add ice cubes and shake well—hard enough to crush the mint on the ice in your shaker. Strain the contents into a chilled cocktail glass or over crushed ice in a large tumbler.

To garnish, use a Microplane to grate a pinch of whole nutmeg across the surface of the cocktail.

LA PETITE MORT

WHAT IF AN EGG cream did, in fact, include egg? We'd wind up with something closer to nineteenth-century fizz cocktail recipes like this one, which plays on two more historic beverages—the Orange Julius and the Bronx cocktail. It's almost as delicious without the booze; just leave out the gin and vermouth, pour it into a shorter Collins glass and top with a splash more soda.

SERVES 1

2 ounces gin, preferably Plymouth or Blue Gin

½ ounce sweet vermouth

1½ ounces fresh orange juice

1 ounce almond milk

½ ounce simple syrup

2 drops pure vanilla extract

1 large egg

Ice cubes

Soda water

In a cocktail shaker, combine the gin, vermouth, orange juice, almond milk, simple syrup, vanilla, and egg. Shake once, hard! Open the shaker, add ice cubes and shake more gently for another 10 to 20 seconds. Strain into a tall Pilsner glass with a couple of ice cubes. Top the glass with soda water and stir a few times to mix it in. Add a straw and drink up.

BROOKLYN CRICKET

THE BROOKLYN EGG CREAM, a mix of chocolate, seltzer, and milk, is an iconic fountain drink that famously contains neither eggs nor cream. It inspired this cocktail, which comes off like a boozy sundae and makes an excellent way to end a meal.

SERVES 1

1½ ounces cream liqueur, preferably
    Caribbean rum cream

¾ ounce white crème de cacao, preferably
    Giffard

¾ ounce Branca Menta

½ ounce Cherry Heering

1 dash Cecil & Merl Cherry Bitters

Pinch of fine sea salt

Ice cubes

3 ounces seltzer

Combine the cream liqueur, white crème de cacao, Branca Menta, Cherry Heering, bitters, and salt in a cocktail shaker. Add ice cubes and briefly shake. Strain into a tall, 12-ounce Collins glass. Tilt the glass slightly and pour the seltzer off the back of a barspoon, creating a plush, frothy head that nears the rim of the glass. Stir the cocktail well to build up more froth. Add a straw and serve.

COLD HOLLOW CABIN

HARD CIDER IS AN historic American beverage in every way. At times, we drank nearly as much cider as we did water. It follows that we've also made mixed drinks with cider since before the Revolutionary War. I like to double the batch and serve it in a punch bowl. Try freezing a small block of ice with a few cinnamon sticks in a small bread pan the night before and use it to chill the drink as you ladle it out to your guests.

MAKES 4 FULL-SIZE COCKTAILS, OR 8 SHORT DRINKS

6 ounces aged rum

2 ounces Cinnamon Syrup (recipe follows)

2 ounces fresh lime juice

4 ounces non-alcoholic apple cider

8 dashes Angostura bitters

Ice cubes, plus a large block of ice

16 ounces hard or sparkling cider

1 apple, for garnish

1 whole nutmeg

1 cinnamon stick

Combine the rum, syrup, and lime juice equally in 2 or 3 cocktail shakers; add ice cubes and shake briefly. Strain into a chilled punch bowl. Add the non-alcoholic apple cider and bitters, then the block of ice. Top the bowl with the hard cider.

Cut the apple into thin wedges, about ½ inch at their widest point; leave a small cut in the flesh of the apple slices so they can be slipped onto the rims of cocktail glasses.

To garnish, use a Microplane to grate a pinch of the whole nutmeg and cinnamon stick across the surface of the punch; garnish each individual glass of punch with an apple. Ladle the punch into the glasses.

CINNAMON SYRUP

MAKES I CUP

1 cup simple syrup

2 cinnamon sticks

Heat the simple syrup over low heat and steep with 2 cinnamon sticks. Let cool at room temperature for 2 hours. Store the syrup with the cinnamon sticks in a sealed glass jar in the refrigerator for up to 2 weeks.

THE PALMER LEGARE

THIS COCKTAIL IS A nod to Arnold Palmer's combination of tea and lemonade, based on a tea-infused gin. To mix things up, try topping off the drink with a spicy ginger beer or dry sparkling wine instead of soda.

SERVES 2

2 grams loose-leaf Earl Grey tea
(or 1 sachet of packaged tea)

3 ounces gin

Ice cubes

Soda water

4 or 5 hulled fresh strawberries

1 ounce simple syrup

1 ounce fresh lemon juice

In a small bowl or cup, combine the tea and gin for 18 minutes. Time it! Over-steeping will make the gin dry, bitter, and tannic.

Fill two 12-ounce Collins glasses with ice cubes and add 2 ounces of soda water to each. In a cocktail shaker, muddle the strawberries, reserving two for garnish. Add the simple syrup, lemon juice, the tea-infused gin, and ice cubes and shake well. Strain into the Collins glasses, topping with additional soda to taste.

To garnish, cut the remaining strawberries in half, then cut vertically halfway up from the tip of the fruit. Use this thin slot to wedge the berries on the rim of the glass. Add a straw and serve.

PART FIVE

SWEETS

Perfect Ripeness

May suitable doses of guaranteed sensual pleasure and slow, long-lasting enjoyment preserve us from the contagion of the multitude who mistake frenzy for efficiency

THE SLOW FOOD MANIFESTO

In my yard upstate, wild blackberries and strawberries grow everywhere. It's a tease watching them ripen. Just as they become perfectly ripe, birds swoop down and snatch them. Since they don't have the luxury of going to the market and getting fresh berries year-round, I can understand why they wait for the moment they reach their peak.

Choosing perfectly ripe, flavorful fruits and vegetables can be tricky. We eat with our eyes, but we taste with our palate and nose. Bruised, soft, browning pears can be perfectly ripe, juicy, and sweet, but still be passed over for the perfect-looking specimen. The first few times you go to the farmers' market, buy organic, or look inside a CSA box, you might be shocked at the "warts and all" appearance of the produce—but know that much of the produce that has been bred to look perfect in the store has actually lost much of its flavor. Beauty, in this case, is more than skin deep.

There are a few factors I consider when choosing produce. First and foremost, I taste, which means getting a sample. Appearance is another consideration. Lush-looking greens on root vegetables like carrots and beets are a welcome sign. There's a little fresh dirt on them? Great. Check the point where the plant was cut. Does it look fresh or brown and dry? That tells you how long ago it was harvested. Compare the stems on two heads of lettuce—one each from the supermarket and the farmers' market. It's revealing.

Give produce, spices, meat, and fish a good sniff. If you can't do this because of packaging, that's a signal to look for a fresher, less-processed product. Ingredients should smell fresh, like flavors you want to have in your food. Tomatoes should have that funky, nightshade, viney scent; apples should be sweet and floral; fish should smell like the ocean.

Sometimes we forget that fruits and vegetables were once growing plants. The belly button, the point where the produce was once connected to the plant and earth, tells you a lot. Smelling that point should give you the subtle aroma of the deliciousness inside.

Feel for weight and firmness. Fruits and root vegetables should be heavy and dense. Crack a piece of asparagus or carrot in half, and it should be almost dripping with moisture. Lettuces should feel light and tight, like a giant budding flower, with no decay on the outer leaves.

Use your instincts and act like a bird picking the ripest berry. You'll develop a sixth sense for choosing ingredients if you tune in, just as you will with cooking and tasting. ❧

LEMON AND BLUEBERRY TART

THERE ARE A BUNCH of steps in this recipe, but don't let that deter you. It's worth it for the incredibly vibrant colors and taste of this zesty, sweet dessert. Tart blueberries balance the sugar in the curd, and the yuzu adds a complex citrus flavor—you can't pinpoint it, but you know there's more than lemon going on. This is a good one to make ahead for a summer dinner party when local blueberries are in season.

MAKES 1 (9-INCH) TART · ACTIVE: 30 MIN · TOTAL: 2 HR

For the crust:

1¼ cups finely ground cornmeal

1¼ cups rolled oats

½ cup almond flour

¼ cup sugar

Pinch of fine sea salt

1½ sticks (12 tablespoons) unsalted butter, cut into small pieces and chilled

2 large eggs

2 teaspoons pure vanilla extract

For the curd:

6 tablespoons unsalted butter, softened

1 cup sugar

2 large eggs

2 large egg yolks

½ cup freshly squeezed lemon juice

2 tablespoons freshly squeezed yuzu juice (or lime juice)

1 teaspoon finely grated lemon zest

For the blueberry topping:

2 tablespoons blueberry jam

2 cups fresh blueberries

1 tablespoon finely sliced fresh spearmint

Preheat the oven to 350°F. Lightly butter a 9-inch tart or pie pan.

To make the crust: In a food processor with the blade attachment, spin the cornmeal, oats, almond flour, sugar, and salt until the oats are finely chopped. Add the butter and pulse until the mixture is mealy.

Add the eggs and vanilla and pulse until the mixture starts to come together. Shape it into a ball, put it between two sheets of parchment paper, and use a rolling pin to roll it into a circle about 10½ inches in diameter.

{ RECIPE CONTINUES }

Chill the dough for 10 minutes. Remove the top sheet of parchment and flip the circle into the center of the tart pan. Press the crust into the pan, working from the center and pressing outward. Cut away any excess dough that hangs over the edges. Bake until the crust is golden brown, about 20 minutes. Make sure it's completely cooked, because it won't be baked again. Set aside to cool.

While the crust bakes, make the curd. In a stand mixer fitted with the paddle attachment, mix together the butter and sugar on low speed until creamy, about 2 minutes. Add the eggs and egg yolks one at a time, mixing until each one is combined. Mix in the lemon and yuzu juices. The mixture will look separated, but it'll come together when you heat it up.

Transfer the mixture to a double boiler and heat over medium heat until the butter starts to melt. Stir constantly until the custard thickens up and reaches 170°F. Stir in the lemon zest and transfer to a bowl. Scatter a few additional small pieces of butter on the curd to prevent a skin from forming. Fill a larger bowl with ice and a little water and set the bowl of curd into it. Let it sit just until cool. If making this ahead of time, the curd can be stored in the refrigerator for up to 3 days. For extra insurance against the curd forming a skin, press plastic wrap or parchment paper against the surface.

To make the topping: Melt the blueberry jam in a small saucepan over low heat. Turn off the heat and stir in the blueberries and spearmint. Let cool.

Whisk the cooled curd until it's smooth. Spread it evenly in the cooked tart crust. Let set in the refrigerator for 15 minutes. Gently pour the blueberries over the curd. Chill for 20 minutes or until set.

RASPBERRY-STUFFED BRIOCHE FRENCH TOAST

I'VE BEEN MAKING THIS dish since my first cooking job when I was 15. Somewhere along the way, I started to serve it as dessert with vanilla ice cream with great success. It works especially well as a finale to a holiday brunch. When berries are at their summer peak, you could use fresh fruit combined with a little honey instead of the preserves.

SERVES 8 · ACTIVE: 15 MIN · TOTAL: 30 MIN

1 loaf Brioche (page 283) or challah bread, chilled

8 ounces cream cheese, cubed and softened

½ cup raspberry preserves

2 large eggs

1 cup heavy cream or whole milk

¼ teaspoon ground cinnamon

¼ teaspoon pure vanilla extract

4 tablespoons unsalted butter

Maple syrup, for serving

4 mint sprigs

½ cup fresh raspberries

Preheat the oven to 325°F.

Using a serrated knife, trim the ends from the loaf of bread (save them for bread crumbs) and slice the loaf into four 2-inch-thick slices. Cut down the middle of the top of each slice, almost all the way, leaving an inch connected at the bottom.

Combine the cream cheese and preserves in a bowl or in a stand mixer fitted with the paddle attachment. Evenly spread 2 to 3 tablespoons of the raspberry cream cheese in the pocket of each slice of bread. (This can be made 1 day ahead and refrigerated.)

Whisk together the eggs, heavy cream, cinnamon, and vanilla in a large baking dish. Dredge the stuffed brioche slices in the batter for about 10 seconds on each side and drain the excess liquid.

Heat 2 tablespoons of the butter in a large skillet over medium heat. Add 2 stuffed brioche slices and cook on both sides until lightly golden brown, 2 to 3 minutes per side. Repeat with the remaining butter and stuffed bread. Transfer the browned French toasts to a nonstick baking sheet and bake until the center filling is hot, about 10 minutes. Cut on the diagonal and serve with maple syrup, mint sprigs, and fresh raspberries.

STRAWBERRY-ALMOND CAKE

with Jasmine Tea

THIS LIGHT, FLUFFY, AROMATIC cake happens also to be gluten-free because it uses almond flour as its base. Jasmine tea brings out the perfume of the strawberries and complements the sweet white chocolate. Be sure to use a good-quality bar of white chocolate made with cocoa butter, not the chips that are mostly milk, oil, and way too much sugar.

SERVES 10 TO 12 · ACTIVE: 30 MIN · TOTAL: 1 HR 30 MIN

Unsalted butter, for greasing the pan

6 ounces white chocolate, chopped

¾ cup heavy cream

1 tablespoon jasmine tea leaves

8 large eggs, yolks and whites separated

1 cup granulated sugar

2 cups almonds, finely ground in a food processor

1 pound strawberries, stemmed and quartered

3 tablespoons confectioners' sugar

2 tablespoons white wine, preferably Riesling

Position a rack in the center of the oven and preheat the oven to 325°F. Line a 10-inch non-stick springform pan with parchment paper and lightly butter it. Place it on a baking sheet.

Bring a saucepan of water to a simmer over low heat. Set a stainless steel bowl over (but not touching) the water. Melt the white chocolate in the bowl. Let cool to room temperature.

In a small pot over low heat, bring the heavy cream and tea leaves to a simmer, then turn off the heat and let steep for 10 minutes.

In a stand mixer fitted with the paddle attachment, beat the egg yolks and ½ cup of the sugar on high speed until it doubles in volume, about 5 minutes.

Stir the ground almonds into the cooled chocolate. Strain the cream through a fine-mesh sieve and add the cream to the chocolate. Gently fold the egg yolks into the chocolate mixture.

In a clean bowl, whisk the egg whites on high speed in the stand mixer until they reach the soft peak stage, just starting to hold onto the whisk. Reduce the speed to low and add the remaining ½ cup sugar. Return to high speed and whip until they're just stiff and glossy. Fold one-third of the whites into the chocolate at a time until just incorporated, being careful not to over-fold the mixture and lose volume.

Pour the batter into the springform pan and transfer the baking sheet to the oven. Bake for about 1 hour. The cake will rise and crack a little, and it's done when a cake tester inserted in the center of the cake comes out clean.

While the cake bakes, toss the strawberries with the confectioners' sugar and wine in a bowl, and let marinate for 20 minutes.

Let the cake cool to room temperature on a rack. Remove it from the pan and top each serving with a spoonful of strawberries.

BLACKBERRY-LAVENDER OAT CRUMBLE

I CAN THINK OF no dish more heartwarming and satisfying than a fruit crumble. The combination of warm fruit filling capped with a crust of oats and spices is timeless. I add lavender to help conjure the aromas of ripe berries picked from the bush. Blackberries are sturdy and release less moisture than blueberries or strawberries, so they make a thick and jammy filling, which I assist with the addition of tapioca—but you can use ripe peaches, plums, nectarines, or wild blueberries (which contain less moisture than the cultivated varieties).

SERVES 6 · ACTIVE: 20 MIN · TOTAL: 1 HR

For the crumble topping:

1 cup rolled oats

⅓ cup packed light brown sugar

⅓ cup all-purpose flour

¼ teaspoon ground nutmeg

¼ teaspoon ground cinnamon

¼ teaspoon ground coriander

1 stick (8 tablespoons) unsalted butter, cut into pieces and chilled

For the berry filling:

⅓ cup granulated sugar

2 tablespoons tapioca pearls

1 teaspoon dried lavender

7 cups fresh blackberries

2 tablespoons unsalted butter, cut into small pieces

Position a rack in the center of the oven and preheat the oven to 350°F.

To make the crumble topping: Spin the oats, brown sugar, flour, nutmeg, cinnamon, and coriander in a food processor just to combine. Add the cold butter and pulse until the mixture has a crumbly consistency, about 5 quick pulses. Don't overmix or you'll have a paste.

To make the filling: In a blender, blend the granulated sugar, tapioca, and lavender until it is a fine powder.

Toss the blackberries with the sugar mixture and pour into a 6 x 9-inch baking dish or 6 individual 8-ounce ramekins. Scatter the butter over the berries, then spread the crumble topping evenly over the top.

Set the baking dish on a baking sheet and bake until the crumble is golden brown and the filling is lightly bubbling around the edges, about 30 minutes (or about 20 minutes if using ramekins). If it's browned but not bubbling, cover with aluminum foil and put it back in the oven for a few more minutes. Let cool for a few minutes, and serve warm.

DULCE DE LECHE CHEESECAKE
with Sea Salt and Caramelized Apples

WHEN I WAS A pastry assistant in high school, cheesecake was one of the first things I learned to make. I haven't stopped making it since! It's an iconic Brooklyn dessert, and one that has been on the James dessert menu since day one, so it's safe to say I'm pretty sentimental about cheesecake. This salty-sweet dulce de leche version is a favorite on Valentine's Day, and I've made it even more decadent by giving it a caramel apple spin. If you can't find graham cracker flour, make your own by finely blending whole graham crackers in a food processor.

SERVES 8 TO 10 · ACTIVE: 45 MIN · TOTAL: ABOUT 5 HOURS, PLUS OVERNIGHT FOR CHILLING

1 (8-ounce) can sweetened evaporated milk

12 ounces cream cheese, cubed and softened

½ cup granulated sugar

12 ounces whole-milk ricotta cheese

4½ ounces crème fraîche

3 large eggs

1½ cups graham cracker flour

¼ cup packed light brown sugar

6 tablespoons unsalted butter, melted

Coarse sea salt, preferably fleur de sel

1 lemon

2 apples, cored and cut into 12 wedges each

½ cup confectioners' sugar

Bring a saucepan of water to a simmer. Place the can of evaporated milk in the simmering water and simmer for 3 hours, adding more water as needed to keep the can covered with water to promote slow, even heat to caramelize the sugar in the milk. Remove and set aside to cool.

Position a rack in the center of the oven and preheat the oven to 325°F.

In a stand mixer fitted with the paddle attachment, beat together the cream cheese and granulated sugar on low speed until smooth. Scrape down the paddle and sides of the bowl.

Add the ricotta and crème fraîche and beat until combined. Scrape down the bowl and beat in the eggs one at a time. Scrape down the bowl again. Open the can of evaporated milk (it should look like caramel inside), reserve 2 tablespoons, and pour the rest into the mixer bowl. Beat on low speed until completely combined, about 2 minutes. Let the batter sit at room temperature while you make the crust.

In a medium bowl, combine the graham cracker flour and brown sugar. Pour in the melted butter and combine with your fingers. Transfer the mixture to the center of a 9-inch springform pan and press evenly onto the bottom and about 2½ inches up the sides of the pan to form a crust.

Pour the batter slowly into the center of the pan, being careful not to disturb the crust. Bake until the center of the cake is firm and a cake tester or skewer inserted in the center comes out clean, about 45 minutes. Let cool at room temperature for 1 hour.

Loosely cover the pan with aluminum foil and place in the refrigerator overnight (for at least 8 hours) to chill completely. Remove the springform pan sides by running a metal spatula or knife around the edge and releasing the spring. Drizzle the reserved 2 tablespoons dulce de leche on top of the cake, then evenly sprinkle 1 tablespoon salt over it.

For the apple topping, heat a large skillet over medium heat. Cut the lemon in half and rub the apple wedges over the lemon, lightly coating them with lemon juice. Sift the confectioners' sugar over the apples, coating the cut sides. Cook the apples cut side down for 5 to 10 seconds on each side, until the sugar bubbles and browns. Transfer the apples to a bowl, season with a pinch of salt, and let cool. Serve a few caramelized apple wedges with each slice of cake.

SAFFRON YOGURT CHERRY PARFAIT

SUNBURST-COLORED YOGURT, BRIGHT RED cherries, and flashes of green from pistachios and mint make this a stunner of a dessert. And the best part is that there's not much work involved in creating it. Saffron doesn't come cheap, but it's so fragrant that you only need a few threads. Seek out Spanish or Indian saffron, both of which have a strong floral flavor.

SERVES 4 TO 6 · ACTIVE: 20 MIN · TOTAL: 2 HR 30 MIN

¼ cup milk

10 saffron threads

¼ cup honey

3 cups full-fat Greek yogurt

2 cups fresh cherries, pitted and halved

2 tablespoons chopped fresh mint, preferably orange mint, plus 4 to 6 sprigs for garnish

¼ cup chopped roasted pistachios

Heat the milk with the saffron threads in a small saucepan over low heat until the milk comes to a simmer. Remove from the heat. Let it cool to room temperature.

In a bowl, whisk the saffron milk and honey with the yogurt and let sit for 10 minutes to infuse the milk and yogurt with the saffron.

Spoon the saffron yogurt into four to six 8-ounce glass serving dishes or parfait glasses and chill for 2 hours to allow the yogurt to firm up.

While the yogurt chills, combine the cherries and mint in a bowl and let macerate for at least 30 minutes.

Spoon the cherries over the chilled yogurt. Top with chopped pistachios and garnish each serving with a mint sprig.

CHOCOLATE AND CHERRY DEVIL CAKE

THIS CAKE IS TENDER and moist, with an airy, light crumb that's developed by aerating the eggs and baking it in a low oven. Chocolate meets the tart pop of cherries in this version, but I've also enjoyed dried apricots soaked in white wine as a topping. You can simplify it further by skipping the glaze and fruit and just giving it a little whipped cream. To make it a bigger splurge, coat the cake in buttercream frosting instead of the glaze.

SERVES 8 · ACTIVE: 1 HR · TOTAL: 2 HR 45 MIN

For the cake:

1 stick (8 tablespoons) unsalted butter, plus more for greasing the pan

8 ounces semisweet chocolate, chopped

6 large eggs, separated

⅔ cup sugar

For the glaze:

⅓ cup heavy cream

3 ounces dark or semisweet chocolate, chopped

For the cherry topping:

½ cup dried cherries

½ cup red wine

⅛ teaspoon ground cinnamon

Position a rack in the center of the oven and preheat the oven to 300°F.

Prepare an 8-inch springform pan by lining the bottom with parchment paper and buttering the sides and the top of the parchment.

To make the cake: Simmer a few inches of water in a medium saucepan. Place a large metal or heatproof glass bowl on top of the pan, making sure the bowl fits snugly and doesn't touch the simmering water. Add the butter and chocolate to the bowl and stir occasionally with a spatula until smooth and melted. Remove from the heat and let cool to room temperature.

In a stand mixer fitted with the paddle attachment, beat the egg yolks and ⅓ cup of the sugar on high speed until the mixture is pale and light and about double the original volume, about 5 minutes. Fold one-third of the yolk mixture at a time into the cooled chocolate until all is incorporated.

In a clean bowl, whisk the egg whites in the mixer on high speed until foamy. Add the remaining ⅓ cup sugar and whisk on high speed until the egg whites are glossy and firm, 3 to 5 minutes. Fold one-third of the whites at a time into the chocolate mixture until just combined.

Pour the batter into the prepared springform pan and place the pan on a baking sheet. Bake for 25 minutes. Reduce the oven temperature to 250°F and continue baking for another 45 minutes. When a cake tester inserted in the center of the cake comes out clean, remove the pan and let cool at room temperature on a baking rack. The cake will sink while cooling. Release the sides of the springform pan.

To make the chocolate glaze: Melt the heavy cream and chocolate in a saucepan over low heat and stir to combine. Let cool to room temperature.

To make the cherry topping: Combine the dried cherries, wine, and cinnamon in a small saucepan over medium heat. Reduce the wine until just evaporated, about 5 minutes.

Using a cake spatula, carefully remove the bottom of the springform pan and parchment paper and place the cake on a plate. Chill the cake for 5 minutes in the freezer.

Cover a baking rack with parchment paper and transfer the cake to the rack. Pour the chocolate glaze in the center of the cake and use an icing spatula to gently spread the glaze outward from the center, letting the glaze drip down the sides. Evenly glaze the top and all sides. If you don't have enough glaze, use the glaze that has dripped onto the parchment paper. Spread the cherries across the top.

Chill the cake in the refrigerator for 30 minutes, or until the glaze looks dry. Let it come to room temperature before serving.

PEAR UPSIDE-DOWN SKILLET CAKE

HAVE A FEW OVERRIPE or beat-up pears? They just found a home. This is a cozy dessert for chilly months when you're up for baking but want to keep it simple. The ever-reliable cast-iron skillet turns out a cake with a golden, crispy crust and soft, caramelized pears. Have it for breakfast with a cup of coffee, or end a fall meal with a slice topped with a scoop of vanilla ice cream.

MAKES I (8-INCH) CAKE · ACTIVE: 20 MIN · TOTAL: I HR

1½ cups all-purpose flour

1½ teaspoons baking powder

1 teaspoon baking soda

1 teaspoon dried lavender

½ teaspoon fine sea salt

3 ripe pears, preferably Bartlett, peeled and cored

2 sticks (1 cup) unsalted butter, softened

⅔ cup granulated sugar

½ teaspoon pure vanilla extract

2 large eggs

½ cup well-shaken buttermilk

¼ cup whole milk

½ cup packed light brown sugar

Preheat the oven to 325°F.

In a medium bowl, sift together the flour, baking powder, baking soda, lavender, and salt. Cut each pear into 8 wedges and roughly dice 1 stick (8 tablespoons) of the butter.

In a stand mixer fitted with the paddle attachment, cream together the granulated sugar and diced butter. Mix in the vanilla. Add the eggs, one at a time, mixing well and scraping down the bowl after adding each one. Alternate between adding one-third of the flour mixture and one-third of the buttermilk, mixing on low speed after each addition, until they're just combined. Pour in the milk and mix again until combined.

Heat the remaining 1 stick (8 tablespoons) butter in a 9-inch skillet over low heat until the foam subsides. Stir in the brown sugar and cook for 3 minutes. Add the pears and cook for 2 minutes, tossing to coat them in the butter and sugar. Remove from the heat and spread the pears in an even layer in the skillet. Spoon the batter over the pears and bake until golden brown and a cake tester or toothpick stuck in the center comes out clean, about 45 minutes. Let cool for 10 minutes.

To flip, run a knife around the edge of the cake to loosen it from the skillet. Place a cake platter or large serving plate on top of the skillet and quickly flip the cake onto the platter. Serve warm.

BLOOD ORANGES

with Chocolate and Mint

THIS RECIPE IS ALL about simplicity and quality. Use high-quality dark chocolate and fresh garden-picked mint and the work is already done. The chamomile and honey add an extra sweet floral element (but can be omitted if you're in a rush). Substitute clementines or navel oranges if you can't find blood oranges.

SERVES 4 TO 6 · ACTIVE: 15 MIN · TOTAL: 15 MIN

½ cup freshly squeezed orange juice

1 chamomile tea bag

2 tablespoons orange blossom honey

6 to 8 blood oranges, peeled and segmented

3-ounce piece dark chocolate (66% cacao or higher)

½ cup fresh mint leaves, preferably orange mint, sliced

Heat the orange juice in a small saucepan over high heat. When it's hot, take it off the heat, add the tea bag, and let steep for 4 minutes. Remove the tea bag and stir in the honey. Chill in the refrigerator until it reaches room temperature.

In a large serving bowl, toss the blood orange segments with the tea-infused orange juice. With a vegetable peeler, shave the chocolate over the fruit. Garnish with the mint. Serve slightly chilled so the chocolate shavings stay firm.

CHOCOLATE BUNDT CAKE

with Cardamom and Orange

WITH THE SIMPLE ADDITION of cardamom and orange zest, this ordinary Bundt cake takes on an exotic "spice market" aroma. Cardamom is a powerfully fragrant but underused spice; it's also thought to be an aphrodisiac, so when you pair it with chocolate, look out.

SERVES 8 TO 10 · ACTIVE: 20 MIN · TOTAL: I HR 30 MIN

2 cups heavy cream

6 ounces semisweet chocolate, chopped

2¼ cups cake flour, plus more for the pan

¾ cup unsweetened Dutch processed cocoa powder, preferably Valrhona

2 teaspoons ground cardamom

1½ teaspoons baking powder

½ teaspoon baking soda

2 tablespoons finely grated orange zest

3 sticks (1½ cups) unsalted butter, cubed, plus more for greasing the pan

2¼ cups sugar

5 large eggs

Preheat the oven to 325°F. Butter and flour a large Bundt pan.

Bring the cream to a simmer in a large saucepan over medium heat. Turn off the heat and stir in the chocolate until it's completely melted and combined. Let cool to room temperature.

Sift together the flour, cocoa powder, cardamom, baking powder, and baking soda. Add the orange zest, coating it evenly with the flour mixture.

In a stand mixer fitted with the paddle attachment, cream the butter and sugar until smooth and well combined, about 5 minutes. Add the eggs one at a time, mixing on low speed after each addition until combined. Add one-third of the flour to the mixer, followed by one-third of the chocolate ganache, and continue alternating between the two, incorporating each addition before adding the next.

Pour the batter into the prepared pan. Bake until a cake tester or toothpick inserted in the center comes out clean, about 1 hour. Let cool on a rack, and serve.

BASICS

Set Up for Success

USE THE LARGEST CUTTING BOARD POSSIBLE

Get the largest cutting board you can fit on your counter. Think of it as your culinary desk. I prefer the feel of my knife on wood or bamboo to plastic or resin. I use a damp piece of natural burlap underneath my board to prevent it from slipping when I'm prepping ingredients.

SEEK OUT HIGH-QUALITY POTS AND PANS

I use the same approach for pots and pans that I do with ingredients: Buy the simplest, highest quality I can afford. The simple cast-iron skillet is an inexpensive, indestructible pan that conducts heat well and lasts practically forever. You want cookware that can go from the stovetop right into the oven, so steer clear of anything with plastic, synthetic, or wood handles.

SEASON YOUR POTS, PANS, AND GRILL

Omelets and crepes were cooked for centuries before nonstick pans were around. If you take the time to season your pans, food will rarely stick to the bottom and pans will be easier to clean. Ceramic, enamel, glass, and nonstick coatings shouldn't be seasoned, as it can damage the pan. Steel and iron pans should always be seasoned.

To season a pan, place ¼ cup of inexpensive coarse salt (like kosher salt) in the bottom. With a kitchen towel, scrub the entire inside of the pan, using the salt as an abrasive. This will remove any particles of food and old oil that may be stuck to the pan. Continue to scrub until the salt feels smooth against the bottom of the pan. Wipe out the salt and use it to season other pans until it becomes gray or discolored. Add 2 tablespoons of high-temperature cooking oil, like avocado or coconut, to the pan. Swirl the oil in the pan, coating the bottom and sides, and heat until it just starts to smoke. Remove the pan from the heat and pour the oil into a heatproof container—it can be used a few more times to season pans. Wipe the pan with a kitchen towel. The pan should be shiny and very smooth. If it doesn't feel as slick as a sheet of ice, repeat the process. This should be done every few times you use the pan.

A seasoned grill holds the same importance as a well-seasoned pan. Carbon and burnt food can build up, which makes food stick, decreases conductivity, and imparts bitter flavors. For an outdoor gas or charcoal grill, first scrub your grill clean of any buildup. Next, get your grill hot, as instructed. Make a seasoning rag by rolling a tight-knit, 100% cotton cloth into a cylinder easily picked up with tongs. Tie it with natural butcher twine and lightly soak it in ¼ cup of high-heat cooking oil, such as avocado or safflower oil. The cloth should be lightly saturated, but not dripping with oil. Using tongs, quickly swipe the seasoning rag once down the grill rails. Reuse it until it becomes very dirty.

CUT WITH SHARP BLADES

Regardless of what knife you make your own, if it's not sharp, it won't work. Hand sharpening is better than machine sharpening because your knives won't be ground down as quickly (and so will last longer).

The blades of vegetable peelers, food processors, and blenders are often overlooked. Using a dull peeler is like trying to mow your lawn with a dull mower blade. If they are not sharp, buy new ones.

CALIBRATE YOUR OVEN AND THERMOMETERS

It's important to check the accuracy of your oven and thermometers every few months. For a probe thermometer, the easiest way to do this is to boil water and make sure the thermometer reads 212°F. To check on your oven, buy an inexpensive oven thermometer and use it to compare to the set oven temperature. It should be accurate within 5 degrees. If your oven temperature is off, adjust the temperature accordingly or check with the manufacturer about how to fix it. ❧

Choosing Cooking Oils

Most cooks use too much oil when they sauté and sear food. A thin layer is all you need when using a seasoned pan (see page 276 for how to season a pan). I use a maximum of 1 to 2 tablespoons of oil in a 10-inch sauté pan for searing and sautéing. If the ingredient has a lot of natural fat, like a good steak, or has been marinated in oil, you need even less. For porous ingredients like mushrooms and eggplant that absorb oil while cooking, add a dash if the pan becomes dry.

There are three factors to consider when choosing cooking oils: smoke point, resistance to oxidation, and taste. The first two affect the last, and every type of cooking oil has a different mix of these characteristics. When you heat cooking oil above its smoke point, it begins to burn and can impart an acrid flavor to the food, and it isn't healthy to breathe or digest. Resistance to oxidation determines the stability of the oil and how it breaks down when exposed to heat, light, oxygen, and moisture. This is why oils should be stored in a cool place in dark-colored or opaque airtight containers. The slower the oil oxidizes, the longer it takes for it to turn rancid. Generally, the darker the oil, the more organic material it contains and the quicker it can go rancid.

Oils are extracted using different methods—some chemical, some mechanical. True cold expeller pressing is chemical-free and retains the most flavors and health benefits.

AVOCADO OR COCONUT OIL

These are the best choices for high-heat cooking like pan-frying and sautéing because of their high smoke points. Avocado oil can be slightly fruity, similar to olive oil, because it is pressed from the flesh of the avocado, not the seed. There are generally two types of avocado oil available—unrefined, sometimes called extra-virgin or virgin, and refined. Most of the refined avocado oil hasn't been chemically processed; it's just filtered more. I prefer it to coconut oil, another flavorful high-heat oil, because it's not solid, but coconut oil is a good alternative. Both will improve your high-heat cooking because the temperature in the pan will get hotter before the oil starts to smoke. This also makes it great for pan frying. Because it doesn't break down as easily, quickly straining and reusing it a few times it after frying will let you defray the cost.

OLIVE OIL

I reach for olive oil the most because of the flavor and body it adds to food. Its smoke point is lower than avocado or coconut, but still high enough to cook with. I use only extra-virgin olive oil and keep three varieties in my pantry: one to cook with; a richer, more flavorful one for vinaigrettes and cold sauces; and a high-quality, young extra-virgin oil with a lot of peppery flavor and vegetal notes to drizzle on dishes as a finishing oil. When

olive oil is heated, it loses some of its health benefits and delicate flavor, so it's not worth spending up for it when using it for high-heat cooking.

Fraud is rampant in the world of olive oils. Buy those that are extra-virgin, cold pressed, and organic to ensure there are no harmful chemicals used in the processing.

BUTTER

It's not an oil, but it acts like one. If you melt high-quality butter, you'll have a high-quality, flavorful cooking oil. I recommend using it instead of chemically processed vegetable and nut oils. For high-heat cooking, use clarified butter (also called ghee), from which the milk solids have been removed. Butter made from grass-fed, pastured cows is healthier and has a pleasantly sweet herbaceous flavor. Browned butter adds a rich, nutty element to any dish.

TREE NUT OILS

Your most flavorful options are walnut, almond, hazelnut, and pistachio. They have a low smoke point and a high cost, so don't cook with these. Use them in vinaigrettes and cold sauces, or drizzle over soups and salads for a rich, nutty accent. French nut oils are the best, and their price reflects that. Nut oils are perishable, so check the pressing date and store in the fridge or a cool, dark place.

VEGETABLE OILS

Many conventional cooking oils you find at the supermarket are processed using harmful chemicals like hexane, and many are made from genetically modified crops. Vegetable oils undergo high-heat chemical-extraction processing, which causes them to go rancid. The oils are then deodorized with petroleum-based chemicals so that they don't smell so bad—but they can be carcinogenic and leave an unpleasant taste behind. Choose expeller-pressed, non-GMO high-temperature vegetable and seed oils like canola and sunflower—they are slowly becoming more available and less expensive. They don't add flavor, but they can withstand high heat. ✤

Salt and Pepper

There may be no ingredients used as frequently as salt and pepper, so they deserve special consideration.

Salt granules have different shapes. Size determines how quickly it dissolves, how it feels between your fingers, and just how much of it fits into a teaspoon. I like Himalayan pink salt for the table and fine sea salt to season with while cooking. I find the flavor of kosher salt to be a bit aggressive, but if I do use it, I prefer light, flaky Diamond Crystal. Finish a dish with coarse fleur de sel to add a salty crunch. Maldon sea salt flakes are best for finishing delicate dishes.

A vintage pepper mill on the table is both useful and visual. Freshly ground pepper from a mill is more aromatic and fragrant than pre-ground because the oils that carry much of the subtle flavor deteriorate when they're exposed to air. I like Tellicherry pepper from western India because of its balance between heat and earthiness. White pepper has a cleaner flavor, which results from the outer shell being removed. I encourage you to give freshly ground white pepper a try; it's easy to find. Pepper, like most spices, has a shelf life of around six months for maximum flavor.

Tamari and soy sauce are good condiments for adding both salinity and umami. I prefer tamari over soy because it contains no wheat (gluten) and has richer flavor with less of a harsh, salty edge. Buying organic ensures that the products being used are non-GMO. ❧

AROMATIC SALTS

MAKES ABOUT ½ CUP

CITRUS SALT

1 lemon, lime, or blood orange   ½ cup coarse sea salt

Preheat the oven to 200°F. Line a baking sheet with parchment paper.

Zest the fruit with a sharp vegetable peeler to get ½-inch strips. Remove any white pith from the inside of the zest. Scatter the zest on the prepared baking sheet and place it in the oven for about 5 hours. (Or, microwave it on low power for about 12 minutes.) Grind the dried peel with the salt in a spice grinder until fine. Store in a sealed jar.

HERB SALT

½ cup coarse sea salt   2 tablespoons dried thyme
                                         (lemon thyme, sage, or
                                         rosemary work well too)

Grind the salt and herbs together in a spice grinder until fine. Store in a sealed jar.

PRICKLY ASH SALT

½ cup coarse sea salt   1 tablespoon Szechuan peppercorns

Grind the salt and peppercorns together in a spice grinder until fine. Store in a sealed jar.

VANILLA SALT

1 vanilla bean   ½ cup coarse sea salt

Cut the vanilla bean in half lengthwise. Scrape the vanilla seeds out of the pod and add to the salt (set aside the pod). Grind the salt and seeds together in a spice grinder until combined but the granules are still coarse. Store in a sealed glass jar with the bean pod inside.

BRIOCHE

A LOAF OF BUTTERY brioche is a workhorse in my kitchen: sandwiches, French toast, bread crumbs, toast points for hors d'oeuvres, bread pudding. It's surprisingly easy to make (that is, if you have a stand mixer—it's a bit of a beast otherwise). Experiment with different variations by adding chopped fresh herbs, grated cheddar, chunks of Brie, or crumbled blue cheese—or go in the other direction, adding chocolate, almonds, or dried fruit. If you are up for a classical French preparation, wrap the dough around some cooked French garlic sausage before baking.

MAKES I LOAF · ACTIVE: 30 MIN · TOTAL: 2 HR

¾ cup warm water (90 to 100°F)

1 (¼-ounce) package active dry yeast

¼ cup sugar

7 large eggs, at room temperature, plus 1 egg, beaten, for the egg wash

5 cups all-purpose flour

2 teaspoons fine sea salt

1½ sticks (12 tablespoons) unsalted butter, cut into small pieces and softened

Vegetable oil, for greasing the pan

Stir the water, yeast, and sugar together in a bowl and place in a warm spot for 10 minutes. The mixture should become frothy and bubble a bit.

In a stand mixer fitted with the paddle attachment, beat the 7 eggs and the yeast mixture on medium speed until well combined and a little foamy, about 3 minutes. Reduce the speed to low and add 2½ cups of the flour, about ¼ cup at a time, until fully incorporated. Add the salt. Mix in the butter, about 2 tablespoons at a time, until incorporated. Slowly add the remaining flour in ¼-cup increments. The batter should be slightly sticky and gooey. Remove the bowl from the mixer and cover with a piece of lightly buttered plastic wrap. Set in a warm place until doubled in volume, about 30 minutes.

Oil a 10 x 5-inch loaf pan. Transfer the dough to the pan and let rise until it doubles in size again, about 30 minutes.

Position a rack in the center of the oven and preheat the oven to 400°F.

Brush the top of the dough with the beaten egg and smooth out any rough spots. Bake on the middle rack until the bread is deep golden brown and a cake tester inserted in the center of the loaf comes out clean, about 45 minutes. Let the brioche cool in the pan for 10 minutes, then remove it from the pan.

SAVORY TART CRUST

(Pâte Brisée)

RICH AND BUTTERY WITH a crisp, flaky texture, this is the classic dough for quiche and savory tarts, like my Tomato and Gruyère Tart (page 52). You can easily tweak the flavor by adding chopped rosemary, chives, or other hardy herbs.

MAKES ENOUGH FOR 1 (9-INCH) ROUND TART OR 1 (9 X 13-INCH) TART
ACTIVE: 10 MIN · TOTAL: 40 MIN

1½ cups all-purpose flour
1 teaspoon finely chopped fresh thyme
¼ teaspoon fine sea salt

Freshly ground black pepper
1 stick (8 tablespoons) unsalted butter,
    cut into ¼-inch pieces and chilled
1 large egg yolk

In the bowl of a food processor fitted with the blade attachment, combine the flour, thyme, salt, and four turns of black pepper and pulse to combine. Add the butter and pulse into the flour about 10 times, or until the butter is cut into small pieces and the mixture resembles coarse crumbs.

With the machine running, add 5 tablespoons cold water and the egg yolk and pulse until a ball of dough forms.

Shape the dough into a ball, wrap it in plastic wrap, and set in a cool place to rest for at least 30 minutes before using. The dough can be refrigerated for up to 3 days or frozen for up to 1 month.

LEMON VINAIGRETTE

THIS IS MY HOUSE vinaigrette. It's simple, bright, and works well with all greens.

MAKES ½ CUP · ACTIVE: 5 MIN · TOTAL: 5 MIN

2 tablespoons freshly squeezed
   lemon juice
Pinch of fine sea salt

Freshly ground black pepper
6 tablespoons extra-virgin olive oil

In a bowl, whisk together the lemon juice, salt, and two turns of black pepper. Add the olive oil in a slow stream, whisking constantly until combined. Store in an airtight container in the refrigerator for up to 1 week.

SHERRY-SHALLOT VINAIGRETTE

SHALLOTS AND SHERRY GIVE this richer depth of flavor and body than the simpler lemon vinaigrette. It can stand up to salads that have strong elements like bacon or garlic, and it adds a little tang to roasted vegetables or meats.

MAKES ½ CUP · ACTIVE: 5 MIN · TOTAL: 5 MIN

1 teaspoon finely chopped shallot
2 tablespoons sherry vinegar
1½ teaspoons smooth Dijon mustard
Pinch of fine sea salt

Freshly ground black pepper
3 tablespoons grapeseed oil
3 tablespoons extra-virgin olive oil

In a bowl, whisk together the shallot, vinegar, mustard, salt, and two turns of black pepper. Add the oils in a slow stream, whisking constantly until combined. Store in an airtight container in the refrigerator for up to 1 week.

BALSAMIC VINAIGRETTE

A GOOD BALSAMIC VINAIGRETTE will save you from ever having to chomp through a boring salad. Try it as a marinade, or add a splash to soups or braises.

MAKES ½ CUP · ACTIVE: 5 MIN · TOTAL: 5 MIN

2 tablespoons Balsamico di Modena vinegar

1 teaspoon smooth Dijon mustard

Pinch of fine sea salt

Freshly ground black pepper

¼ cup extra-virgin olive oil

2 tablespoons grapeseed oil

In a bowl, whisk together the vinegar, mustard, salt and two turns of black pepper. Add the oils in a slow stream, whisking constantly until combined. Store in an airtight container in the refrigerator for up to 1 week.

BALSAMIC REDUCTION

THIS SWEET AND SOUR condiment is dynamite drizzled on soups, salads, meats, and grilled bread with olive oil. It's an inexpensive way to replicate pricey aged balsamic vinegars.

MAKES ½ CUP · ACTIVE: 30 MIN · TOTAL: 1 HR 30 MIN

3 cups Balsamico di Modena vinegar

1 garlic clove, peeled and smashed

Pinch of fine sea salt

Fresh black pepper

1 rosemary sprig

In a small pot, heat the balsamic vinegar over low heat, stirring with a whisk every few minutes. When the liquid is reduced by half, add the garlic. Continue cooking until the vinegar has the consistency of honey. Stir in the salt and one turn of freshly ground black pepper and remove the pot from the heat. Strain through a fine-mesh sieve set over a glass bowl. Add the rosemary sprig and set the bowl aside for an hour to cool to room temperature. This will keep in an airtight container in the refrigerator for up to 2 weeks.

CORIANDER-GINGER VINAIGRETTE

TOASTED GROUND CORIANDER AND fresh ginger make this a slightly exotic, warmly flavored vinaigrette. I like it drizzled on fish or tossed into any salad that has citrus in it.

MAKES ABOUT ½ CUP · ACTIVE: 10 MIN · TOTAL: 10 MIN

2 tablespoons ground coriander

2 tablespoons peeled and minced
   fresh ginger

2 teaspoons minced shallot

2 tablespoons rice vinegar

½ teaspoon fine sea salt

6 tablespoons extra-virgin olive oil

Freshly ground black pepper

In a sauté pan over medium heat, toast the coriander, stirring frequently, until it starts to smoke and become fragrant, about 3 minutes. Turn off the heat and add the ginger, shallot, vinegar, and salt. Whisk in the olive oil and a few turns of black pepper. Let cool, and refrigerate in an airtight container for up to 1 week.

WARM GOAT CHEESE FONDUE

THIS IS A QUICK and easy cheese sauce that can be used almost anywhere.

MAKES 1 CUP · ACTIVE: 5 MIN · TOTAL: 10 MIN

1 tablespoon dry white wine

1 teaspoon finely chopped shallots

Pinch of dried thyme

1 cup heavy cream

4 ounces goat cheese, crumbled by hand

½ tablespoon unsalted butter

Fresh black pepper

1 teaspoon thinly sliced chives

In a small saucepan over low heat, reduce the wine with the shallots and thyme until almost fully evaporated, about 2 minutes. Stir in the cream and cook until the sauce has reduced by a third, 3 to 5 minutes. Add the cheese and stir until it's melted and the mixture is smooth. Keep warm. Just before using, stir in the butter, one turn of freshly ground black pepper, and the chives.

ROASTED RED PEPPER SAUCE

THIS SUPER EASY, TANGY sauce livens up simple vegetables, fish, and chicken. If spicy is your thing, add a pinch of red pepper flakes or sliced chile pepper to the blender. Roasting the pepper yourself will give the sauce more flavor, but you can make this with jarred roasted red peppers if you're short on time.

MAKES ABOUT 1½ CUPS · ACTIVE: 10 MIN · TOTAL: 25 MIN

1 red bell pepper

Extra-virgin olive oil

1 garlic clove, finely chopped

1 tablespoon rice vinegar

1 tablespoon unsalted butter

1 tablespoon soy sauce

½ cup hot vegetable stock or water

Fine sea salt

Heat the oven to high broil. If your oven is not equipped with a broiler, preheat to 450°F.

Rub the pepper with oil and place it on a baking pan lined with aluminum foil. On the top oven rack, broil the pepper until the skin begins to blister and turn black and it collapses a bit, about 5 minutes per side. Transfer the pepper to a small bowl and cover with plastic wrap. Let it steam for 5 minutes.

Place the foil from the baking pan on a cutting board, dirty side up. Halve the pepper and pull off the stem. With a knife, scrape off the black, blistered skin. Flip over and scrape out the seeds. Roughly chop the pepper and put it in a blender with the garlic, vinegar, butter, and soy sauce. Add ¼ cup of the vegetable stock and blend until smooth. (Heat the mixture in a small pot if the butter is not fully melted.) The sauce should be thick enough to coat the back of the spoon. Add more stock to adjust the consistency, if needed. Add salt to taste.

BASIC AROMATIC MARINADE FOR MEAT

MAKES ENOUGH FOR 1 TO 2 POUNDS MEAT

¼ cup vegetable oil

1 shallot, thinly sliced

2 garlic cloves, crushed

1 teaspoon whole black peppercorns

1 bay leaf

6 thyme sprigs

Thoroughly dry the meat you are using with a paper towel. Mix all of the ingredients in a bowl with the meat, completely coating all surfaces. Transfer the meat and marinade to an airtight container and refrigerate for up to 5 days. Before using, remove any excess oil and aromatics sticking to the meat.

BASIC AROMATIC MARINADE FOR FISH

MAKES ENOUGH FOR 1 TO 2 POUNDS FISH

¼ cup vegetable oil

1 shallot, thinly sliced

1 garlic clove, crushed

4 whole cloves

¼ teaspoon whole black peppercorns

6 thyme sprigs, preferably lemon thyme
(or use regular thyme and the zest of
1 lemon peeled in large pieces)

Mix all of the ingredients together in a bowl with the fish you are using, completely coating all surfaces. Transfer the fish and marinade to an airtight container and refrigerate for up to 5 days. Before using, remove any excess oil and aromatics sticking to the fish.

BASIC ACIDIC MARINADE FOR RED MEAT

MAKES ENOUGH FOR I TO 2 POUNDS RED MEAT OR GAME

¼ cup dry red wine

2 garlic cloves, crushed

1 teaspoon whole black peppercorns

3 thyme or rosemary sprigs

Thoroughly dry the meat with a paper towel. Mix all of the ingredients together in a bowl with the meat, completely coating all surfaces. Transfer the meat and marinade to an airtight container and refrigerate for up to 5 days. Before using, remove any excess oil and aromatics sticking to the meat.

VEGETABLE STOCK

MAKING VEGETABLE STOCK IS fairly speedy—it only needs about 1 hour to simmer. That's long enough to extract the vegetal flavors, but not so long that it ends up bitter. I like adding wine to stocks because it brings acidity and body. The turnip, not a vegetable you usually see in stock, adds a deep, mellow flavor.

MAKES 4 TO 6 CUPS · PREP: 20 MIN · TOTAL: 1 HR 20 MIN

2 carrots, peeled and cut into ½-inch pieces (about 1 cup)

2 celery stalks, cut into ½-inch pieces (about 1 cup)

1 onion, cut into large dice (about 1 cup)

1 leek, cut into large dice (about 2 cups)

1 medium white turnip, peeled and cut into ½-inch pieces (about 1 cup)

¼ teaspoon fine sea salt

2 cups dry white wine (a Sauvignon Blanc or other non-oaky wine)

1 bay leaf

1 thyme sprig

1 teaspoon whole black peppercorns

Combine the carrots, celery, onion, leek, turnip, salt, and 8 cups cold water in a large stockpot. Bring to a simmer over medium heat.

Skim off any foam or impurities that float to the top. Add the wine, bay leaf, thyme, and peppercorns. Return to a simmer, and cook for 1 hour.

Strain the stock through a fine-mesh sieve set over a large bowl; discard or compost the solids. Let the stock cool before storing in an airtight glass container. It will keep for up to 5 days in the refrigerator or up to 3 months in the freezer.

CHICKEN STOCK

THIS IS A STRAIGHTFORWARD, use-in-everything kind of chicken stock. For a version that's especially well suited to braising, roast the chicken pieces and vegetables at 350°F until golden brown before adding them to the stockpot.

MAKES ABOUT 2 QUARTS · ACTIVE: 30 MIN · TOTAL: 4 HR

1 (3½-pound) chicken, with giblets (no liver), cut into 8 pieces (drumsticks, thighs, breasts, wings)

2 onions, quartered

2 medium carrots, cut into 2-inch pieces

1 celery stalk, cut into 2-inch pieces

3 garlic cloves, crushed

Fine sea salt

½ cup dry white wine

4 flat-leaf parsley sprigs

4 thyme sprigs

1 teaspoon whole black peppercorns

1 bay leaf

Put the chicken pieces into a large stockpot. Add cold water to cover by about 2 inches and bring to a boil over medium heat. Immediately reduce the heat to a low simmer. Skim any froth or solids that rise to the top. Add the onions, carrots, celery, garlic, and a pinch of salt, and return to a simmer. Add the wine, parsley, thyme, peppercorns, and bay leaf, and continue to simmer for 2 hours and 30 minutes, occasionally skimming any solids, fat, or foam that rises to the top.

Remove from the heat and let the stock sit for 5 minutes to settle. Skim once more, then strain it through a fine-mesh sieve set over a large bowl. Let the stock cool before storing in an airtight glass container or containers. It will keep for up to 1 week in the refrigerator or up to 2 months in the freezer.

The Best Ingredients

Americans spend a lower percentage of income on food than any other developed nation. We are experts at producing cheap food using industrial farming methods. Most of the ingredients produced in this way are inferior in taste and nutrition to hand-crafted, small-batch-produced ingredients.

If you think the farm-to-table movement is for a bunch of aging hippies and elitists who have a lot of extra income to spend, fine. If politics and sustainability aren't driving forces for you, no problem. Buy fresh, local sustainable ingredients because they taste better. Buy them for your ego so you can boast to friends by naming seven different kinds of heirloom tomatoes in the salad you made. Buy them because the volunteers helping at the farmers' market booths are cute. Go to the farmers' market or butcher, spice shop, and fish store because you hate walking down those long supermarket aisles on bad linoleum floors under glaring fluorescent lights.

Ask yourself if you can feel a connection to the food you buy. The time you invest at the farmers' market and artisanal food shops will be less than the time you'll spend trying to make bland, poor-quality food taste good. ❖

ONLINE FOOD RETAILERS

redbee.com *Artisanal honey*

murrayscheese.com *Cheese, oil, vinegars, gourmet products*

dartagnan.com *Mushrooms, meat, poultry*

almagourmet.com *Cheese, meats, mushrooms, oils, vinegars*

kalustyans.com *Spices, Indian ingredients*

katagiri.com *Japanese specialty items*

brooklynbrine.com *Pickles*

acmesmokedfish.com *Smoked fish*

pierlessfish.com/collections *Fresh fish and seafood*

brownetrading.com *Fresh fish and seafood*

debragga.com *Meat and poultry*

chefswarehouse.com *Wide variety of ingredients*

truefoodsmarket.com *Spices, flours, organic products*

latourangelle.com *Artisanal oils*

spectrumorganics.com/spectrum-naturals *Oils*

slowfood.com *Slow Food movement*

CLASSES, GARDENING, AND FOOD INFORMATION

stonebarnscenter.org *Stone Barns Center for Food and Agriculture*

bbg.org *Brooklyn Botanical Garden*

urbanhomestead.org *Urban homesteading info*

seedsofchange.com *Seeds and garden supplies*

dirtdoctor.com *Organic gardening blog and products*

nativeseeds.org *Native American seeds*

compostguide.com *Composting information*

fieldforest.net *Mushroom growing supplies*

snug-harbor.org *Horticulture and composting*

eomega.org *Seminars on sustainability*

soiltest.uconn.edu *Soil testing*

soilhealth.cals.cornell.edu *Soil testing*

ewg.org *Environmental Working Group*

eatwellguide.org *Sustainable food sources*

seafoodwatch.org *Sustainable Seafood Guide*

nongmoshoppingguide.com *Non-GMO food guide*

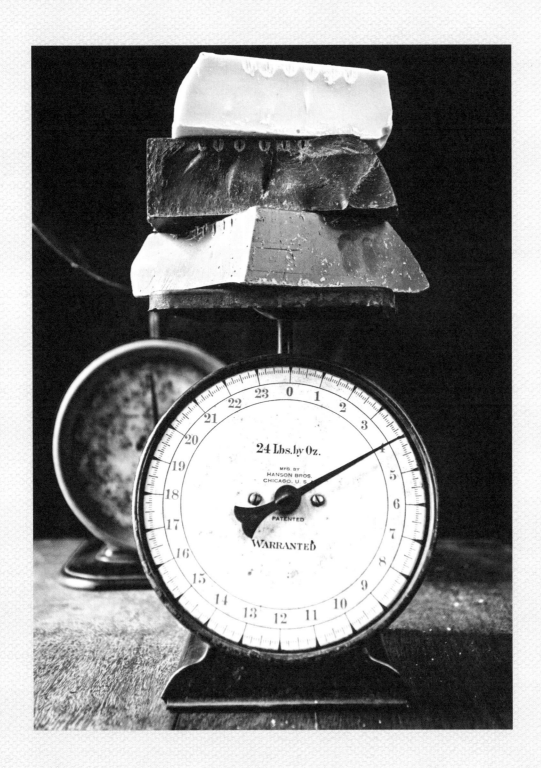

ACKNOWLEDGMENTS

Make me sweet again,
Fragrant and fresh and wild,
And thankful for any small event.

RUMI

I AM GRATEFUL TO all the friends, clients, chefs, recipe testers, and family who supported me along this journey, especially: Deborah Williamson; Alia Hanna Habib; Michael Szczerban; Alex Oefeli; Ed Anderson; Matt Long; Tammy Walker; Laura Palese; Michael Sand; Garrett McGrath; everyone at Little, Brown and Company; Natalie Chitwood; Rachel McKinstry; Justin Lane Briggs; Matthew Stucky; Mom, Dad, Jason, and Lynette; Bonnie and Daniel Shapiro; Robert and Heidi Korngut; David Korngut, Esq.; the Calvert family; the Shapiro family; Agnes Gund; Georgia and Fisher; Bill Wilson; Andrew Garcon; All those who have been apart of the James restaurant crew, with special thanks to the long timers Virgie, Clay, Juan, Geronimo, and Dustin; Mario Manzano and family; Jaya; Elliot Jurist; and Robert Creal.

Thank you.

PHOTOGRAPHY CREDITS

Deborah Williamson: 1, 2, 10 (top and bottom left), 12, 17 (top), 27, 37, 38, 49, 67, 76, 88, 91, 116, 126, 142, 261

Ed Anderson: 5, 15, 17 (bottom), 18, 21, 24, 28, 29, 41, 42, 45, 50, 53, 57, 62, 65, 69, 79, 83, 84, 87, 92, 96, 99, 102, 105, 106, 118, 124, 128, 130, 134, 135, 141, 154, 157, 159, 164, 168, 172, 182, 185, 190, 195, 197, 200, 203, 211, 215, 217, 230, 233, 236, 239, 240, 243, 244, 247, 248, 250, 253, 263, 267, 272, 275, 276, 279, 280, 282

Matt Long: 10 (bottom right), 34, 58, 61, 70, 75, 108, 111, 115, 120, 123, 133, 145, 146, 149, 150, 153, 160, 162, 166, 171, 174, 176, 179, 181, 187, 188, 205, 208, 219, 220, 222, 227, 229, 255, 256, 271, 277, 284, 295

INDEX